Bus
STO

12/6/94

ALLEN COUNTY PUBLIC LIBRARY
FORT WAYNE, INDIANA 46802

You may return this book to any agency, branch,
or bookmobile of the Allen County Public Library.

DEMCO

Also by
Neal H. Olshan, Ph.D.

Phobia Free and Flying High
Depression
Fears and Phobias: Fighting Back
Power Over Your Pain Without Drugs
Everything You Always Wanted to Know About Phobias,
   But Were Afraid to Ask
The Scottsdale Pain Relief Program

Golden Handcuffs

Golden Handcuffs

*How Women Can Break Free
of Financial Dependence
in Their Intimate
Relationships*

Dr. Neal H. Olshan

A BIRCH LANE PRESS BOOK
Published by Carol Publishing Group

Copyright © 1994 by Neal H. Olshan
All rights reserved. No part of this book may be reproduced in any form, except by a newspaper or magazine reviewer who wishes to quote brief passages in connection with a review.

A Birch Lane Press Book
Published by Carol Publishing Group
Birch Lane Press is a registered trademark of Carol Communications, Inc.
Editorial Offices: 600 Madison Avenue, New York, N.Y. 10022
Sales and Distribution Offices: 120 Enterprise Avenue, Secaucus, N.J. 07094
In Canada: Canadian Manda Group, P.O. Box 920, Station U, Toronto, Ontario M8Z 5P9
Queries regarding rights and permissions should be addressed to Carol Publishing Group, 600 Madison Avenue, New York, N.Y. 10022

Carol Publishing Group books are available at special discounts for bulk purchases, for sales promotion, fund-raising, or educational purposes. Special editions can be created to specifications. For details, contact: Special Sales Department, Carol Publishing Group, 120 Enterprise Avenue, Secaucus, N.J. 07094

Manufactured in the United States of America
10 9 8 7 6 5 4 3 2 1

Library of Congress Cataloging-in-Publication Data
Olshan, Neal.
    Golden handcuffs : how women can break free of financial
dependence in their intimate relationships / by Neal H. Olshan.
        p. cm.
    "A Birch Lane Press book."
    ISBN 1-55972-202-9
    1. Women—Finance, Personal. 2. Dependency (Psychology)
I. Title.
HG179.0448   1993
332.024'042—dc20   93-23062
                                                            CIP

To MARY M. OLSHAN. Without her thoughts, comments, criticisms, and insightful writing, *Golden Handcuffs* would never have become a reality

Contents

Preface		11
Acknowledgments		15
1.	It Takes Two to Forge the Golden Handcuffs	19
2.	Do You Wear the Golden Handcuffs?	39
3.	The Rationalization Game	57
4.	The Money Trap	77
5.	Dreams, Goals, and Expectations	91
6.	Assert Yourself	113
7.	Make Changes and Move On	131
8.	Success Stories From the Golden Handcuffs Group	141

Preface

I have been a psychologist in private practice for twenty years, during which time I have witnessed a continuing increase in the number of women who feel both trapped and overly dependent in their relationships with men—a combination that goes beyond what normally is considered psychologically healthy.

Of course, no relationship is completely without *some* dependency. From our first moments of life we depend on others for security, safety, nourishment, and love. As we get older, a portion of this dependency changes, and we learn to provide for at least a fair share of the needs of others. Ideally, dependency in any relationship takes the form of a mutually interactive process that allows for the growth and maturity of both individuals.

Although *no* relationship is perfect (outside of those in some old sitcoms), women and men alike usually learn to adjust to the fluctuating nature of just about *any* sort of relationship. They can, in fact, learn to use dependence with great care—as well they should, since it is like a potent spice that can enhance the food you prepare. If you add too much, or too little, your meal can be ruined. Women who understand the proper and judicious use of positive dependency will much more often than not be privileged to enjoy the best in relationships with men.

I have written this book because for so long a time, week after difficult week, my female patients had been coming to me angry at—and terribly disillusioned with—their relationships. They felt trapped, afraid, anxious, and depressed. They also lacked self-confidence and self-esteem. One of them said it best: "Before coming here, I'd read all the books, watched all the shows from Oprah to Phil, and I still didn't know how to get out of the problem. Now I feel like a prisoner in the relationship with Randy, with no chance to escape!" Another patient added: "I'm sick and tired of not knowing when dependency is good or bad. My confusion is getting worse and I feel guilty all the time. I want answers I can *use*." And so it went.

When it became feasible to do so, I started a group for women trapped by dependency. However, while I had formed a basic outline for the course of therapy, I soon realized that this effort was only the beginning of what became a task requiring years devoted to developing the best possible methods to help these women.

The first meeting of our group was a nervous situation for everyone involved. At the end of this initial session, I asked some of the women what the group should be called. Robin had the first suggestion. She faced Michelle and said "Like you, at first I thought he was giving me a pair of golden bracelets, but now I realize they are only golden handcuffs."

From that moment on, the group was known as the Golden Handcuffs Group.

Every therapy group has a reason for, a purpose to, its existence—a mutual set of psychological or emotional circumstances common to each member's life. This group provided a forum for sharing these situations, identifying common problems therein, and exploring alternatives thereto. It proved a network for both support and growth. Indeed, the Golden Handcuffs Group became the source of true hope for women of all ages and backgrounds.

It takes a lot of work to break the Golden Handcuffs, and the first hard job is admitting that you wear them. In the following chapters you will meet a number of women from the Golden Handcuffs Group. All of their stories are factual. I hope the reciting of their struggles, their failures, and (especially) their successes will be of inspiration to you.

Thank you for having the courage to join us.

Acknowledgments

In the process of conceiving, writing, and editing a book, a number of people always work together to make the final product possible. First and foremost is my wife, Mary. Whenever the road seems unclear, Mary is always there to provide the road map, since I seem inherently incapable of ever asking for directions. As a therapist, Mary is unsurpassed in her ability to help others explore alternatives and gain the courage to make changes. Many of the ideas in this book are based upon Mary's successes in working with women and trying to help them break free of the handcuffs. The other women in my life, my daughters Sam and Mo, are always there for me when I need them. Thanks go to my son, Bob, who when I am not writing, is there to provide the needed "change of pace and distractions." And a very special thanks goes to the best mother and father-in-law in the world, Mary and Ken Walker.

Kevin McDonough, my editor at Birch Lane Press, deserves much credit for his invaluable editorial help and long hours. Edward Novak III, my agent, was always there to help and guide the project. Additional thanks and recognition are extended to Mike Arkush for his assistance.

Finally I must thank the thousands of patients who over the years have taught my staff and me so very much about relationships and human dignity.

Golden Handcuffs

CHAPTER ONE

It Takes Two to Forge the Golden Handcuffs

Michelle, now thirty-four, grew up believing in fairy tales. Ignored by her father and misunderstood by her mother, she bravely struggled through adolescence, clinging to the dream that one day the right man would come and take away all her pain. He would possess everything she read about in her favorite romance novels—good looks, compassion, success. He would show her a new world, much safer than the old one, and they would live happily ever after. Throughout her twenties she waited for her savior. This kept her alive.

Finally, in 1989, she met Brian, and knew instantly he was that man. He bought her flowers and candy, and promised the universe. He vowed that he would work hard to support her while she made babies and took care of the home. He was her *rescuer*—and they were married in a big church ceremony on the happiest day of her life.

But he was not her rescuer. He was her *jailer*. Within three months of their wedding, Brian was no longer her Brian. He was an impostor. Or maybe he was finally his real self—petty, vindictive, unsupportive, and, most of all, a control freak. He felt he had the right to direct every minute of Michelle's life, from what she wore, to the friends she made, to which television shows she watched. Life with Brian almost made her long for her adolescence again, and with it the father who always wished she had been a boy.

For almost three years Michelle suffered in silence. She refused to believe that her childhood fantasies had dissolved into one endless nightmare. She took all the abuse from Brian (mostly verbal) and never fought back. After all, where would she go? She had no marketable skills, and there were two young children to consider. Without Brian's income they would be lost, three more anonymous candidates for the town's homeless shelter. Brian was horrible, all right, but he sure beat the streets.

She even hid the truth from herself, with a clever game of distortions, lies, and excuses. Anything she could invent in her head was better than facing the reality of her own hopelessness. Each time Brian showed a glimpse of that old charm and gentleness, she convinced herself that things would be wonderful again, just as they had been in the courtship days. But, just as suddenly, the new Brian would resurface, his temper worse than ever, and she would get depressed all over again. The pattern was confusing and led to a severe depression.

It Takes Two to Forge the Golden Handcuffs

Then, one day, Michelle came to see me about her back, which she had injured in a minor auto accident. As an expert in chronic pain, I was chosen to give her mental techniques to alleviate the pain. She seemed to respond well. But, as the weeks went by, it became clear that Michelle did not want to talk further about the spasms in her back. It was her whole *life* that was out of joint.

"I used to be a woman. Now, I feel like a slave. I am a slave to the man who was supposed to liberate me from everything. He treats me like a child.

"I can't do anything without his approval, and that's especially true when it comes to money. The other day, I wanted to get sandals for the two girls, but I was afraid to tell him. Because every time I spend a dime, he has a tantrum. He says we can't afford stuff like that, but, it's funny how that standard doesn't apply when he wants to use the money. When he wants to buy anything, he does it and there are no questions asked, period. He says he earns the money and therefore he can do whatever he pleases.

"I don't even know what our economic situation is. He keeps it all to himself. Every time I ask him, he says he'll show me later. And the only time he seems ready to explain it to me on the computer is when he knows that my back hurts me too much for me to get up. He thinks he is being very clever, but I know his game.

"I am trapped. I know I have to get out of this relationship before it kills me, and boy, am I tempted. I have literally jumped in the car, with the kids in the back seat, packing just enough for a few weeks, turned the ignition on, and gotten ready to leave town. But I never leave the driveway. I am too

21

scared. I know he will track me down, and I will not get very far. I just bring the kids back inside and prepare for more abuse, and each time I feel worse about myself. And what really hurts is I know I'm setting a really bad example for my children. They have to see me as weak.

"When I married Brian, he gave me a golden bracelet as our first wedding gift. It was so gorgeous, and I vowed to wear it all the time. For the first time in my life, I was truly happy. But the golden bracelet has turned into golden handcuffs. I hardly ever put that bracelet on anymore, but I don't have to. It's there with me all the time."

Michelle's story is hardly unique. Unfortunately, there are millions of Michelles scattered across the country—once-proud women in stagnating, suffocating relationships they can't escape because they have no money and no skills to survive even adequately with a family to support. Many women, both rich and poor, live with the fear that their lives will change dramatically if they end their relationship or take a firm stand within the confines of the relationship. By allowing their husbands to control every aspect of the couple's finances, they have surrendered their power, and they live essentially as indentured servants. The Golden Handcuffs symbolize their incarceration. Many of these women have all the trappings of ease and comfort, many living in wealth they never could have imagined. But the real cost—their dignity—makes them veritable prisoners in their own homes.

This is hardly a new development in America, and certainly not in other areas of the world. Women have played this role for centuries, desperately hanging on to men they can't tolerate, because the alternative—solitude—seems even more dangerous. And, all along, society has been a willing accomplice, crowning the man as the prime authority, subjugating the woman to permanent lower-class status. Many women have been constantly dependent on one or another man who, they hoped, would be at least a benevolent dictator. Divorce was not permitted by religion or custom. Girls were brought up to be quiet and sweet, and were forbidden to express the kind of anger that boys owned. To be a lady meant being quiet, passive, and "sweet," and if you were to be chosen before the stigma of "old maid" set in, it was important to follow the guidelines.

Well, the times, they are a-changin'. Countless women in the 1990s are tired of being *too* dependent on their domineering husbands, weary from making compromises for economic security. That doesn't mean, however, that they are all courageous enough to do something about it, because the risks they face still are very real. But, at the very least, they are finally beginning to recognize this reality with greater urgency—and *that* is their first step toward fixing the imbalance.

The purpose of this book isn't to solve every woman's problem; that degree of solution will never happen, no matter the effort. What I will do, however, is outline a series of clear warning signals and characteristics which can help determine which women are controlled by the Golden Handcuffs, and provide simple techniques and steps to follow that might liberate them once and for all. This certainly is no magical cure, and not every woman will be able to follow up on these suggestions. (Some may not even apply *to* their situation.) But the time for women to acknowledge their predicament, console each other over bridge, or lunch at the club, and resign themselves to a lifetime of diminished expectations with a man who acts more like a warden, is over. The time for women to *act* has begun—and, hopefully, this book will teach them how.

After Michelle came to see me, there was Janet, and Rachel, and Lynn. And each time the scenario was similar. Presumably, or so they claimed, they showed up at my office looking for ways to alleviate depression resulting from chronic physical pain, anxiety disorders, or phobias: "Dr. Olshan, my back is killing me." "Dr. Olshan, I'm so nervous and frightened all the time and I don't understand why." Certainly I was most eager to make them understand that there are ways to combat the body's weaknesses and to overcome their irrational fears. But each time, after a couple of visits, the women's true motives could no longer be disguised. They could never initiate therapy with the purpose of curing their marriage; that would be far too threatening to them. So, in the beginning, they had to locate a back door, a way to get at the problem without fully acknowledging their dreadful isolation. The most common statement was "I feel so empty, so lonely inside of me."

I noticed that when I gave them a homework assignment, they responded with something like "This will interfere with what my husband is doing." For example, if someone had a driving phobia and needed to practice driving, she would respond: "I'll have to do it while my husband isn't around." In other words, they relied on their husband's approval for their every move. Once, I asked a woman to bring her husband into a session. Alone she was strong, assertive, full of confidence. With him she was a wreck, a child in a woman's body. It was horrible to watch. I could literally see the self-esteem drained from her.

I searched for anything written that might help me give these women some answers. But all I found were feminist manuals that, essentially, declared war against men. And I never felt that *these* women were prepared for waging *that* kind of battle. Sure, they had to stand up for their rights, and no longer accept life as second-class citizens. But they needed to assert themselves boldly *without* choosing hate as the alternative, *without* sacrificing any chance for reconciliation and mutual understanding. Hate would only destroy them!

Each woman who came into my office sincerely believed that she was the only one going through this ordeal. I heard statements like "I must be crazy" and "There must be something wrong with me" and "Why is this only happening to *me?*" There was always a profoundly devastating sense of aloneness, which made them slide even farther into self-pity. I told them that in fact they *weren't* alone—but they didn't quite believe me. So it seemed that the sensible thing to do was to form a support group for women manacled by the Golden Handcuffs.

We met for several years, about half a dozen of us, and there was regular and significant progress. In some cases, the women gained enough understanding even to change the dynamics of their relationships. But I realized that millions of other women *couldn't* afford the luxury of weekly visits to a therapist—and that even if they *had* the money, their husbands would never permit such an intrusion onto male turf.

They would control that matter just like everything else. The only immediate and practical way to reach these women was via the printed page.

Who were (and are) these women, anyway? Well, they are of many types. There are those who boldly set out from the start to acquire tremendous wealth—in common parlance, golddiggers. Usually they are the same females who, all through secondary school, increasingly learned that they could easily manipulate males by using their gorgeous looks and sex appeal. That's how they tend *always* to derive their self-worth and validation. Generation after generation has legions of these women, the ones who invariably go for the temporarily most popular guys and discount the less flashy ones (who nevertheless would probably, sooner or later, make them happier than the flash-in-the-pan type would be prone to).

Typically, these kind of women, despite their allure, really don't believe in themselves. They mistakenly assume that succeeding in this game of capturing the man with the most money, the man who will never stop spoiling them, is the only way that they will like themselves, and that others will look up to them. Surely, if other women are jealous of them, then they must have it good. If they're seen in the right restaurants, then they must be okay. If they drive a Mercedes instead of a Subaru, they must be happy. Right? *Wrong!* Years later, often when it's too late, they realize that the money didn't buy self-respect, but it did buy a fair share of misery.

Then there are the women who thought they selected their husbands out of love, *not* for their bank accounts. Like

Michelle, at first they couldn't have been more satisfied. Prince Charming, their ultimate savior, had arrived to provide for their every need, to compensate for the Daddy who was never really a Daddy. But, for these women, the honeymoon didn't last long. They discovered that their husbands, while not horrible, were not the people they thought they had married. He was interested only in himself, and saw his wife as a trophy to be carried around from one social gathering to another, an affirmation of his own appeal to women. To this type of man, his woman's life always is expected to be sacrificed for *his* good. He seems unable to see others as having points of view or even any rights, especially if they would conflict with his.

Whatever their motives, women who painfully watched their mothers go through the same kind of relationship tend to repeat it. Instead of standing up to their spouses, these Moms took the abuse and did nothing. Their daughters grew up with great sympathy for their mothers, but not much respect, and it was almost inevitable that the pattern would be repeated in the next generation. Such daughters spend much of their lives trying to win over the men their mothers never could.

At first, some women mistake the man's generosity for love: "He's giving me all these flowers; he's buying me these expensive dresses. He loves me. He *loves* me." Not quite. He *needs* you. He needs you to compensate for his own insecurities. He needs you to escape from his own demons, or from the father who was never there for him, or from the nurturing mother who no longer had the energy to play that role. Presto, he gets married, grooming his wife to become his second mother—supportive, reliable, but most of all submissive. Unfortunately, in the beginning of a relationship, she is more likely to want to be everything he desires because she hasn't yet seen the cost of such behavior. When she tries to become an equal partner, he rebels vehemently and accuses her of not being the person he married. He has a point!

But it takes two to create the Golden Handcuffs, and it serves no purpose to automatically lay all the blame on the man. Often the woman is just as responsible. She claims she was searching for love, but, on an intuitive level at least, she was getting exactly what she wanted. She grew up hating herself, either because she, too, didn't get the attention early on from a male authority figure (her father), or perhaps she was molested. A huge percentage of the women in Golden Handcuffs relationships *were* sexually abused, and never spoke out against their perpetrator. Instead they blamed themselves, setting up a pattern of self-hatred that's very difficult to shake.

By choosing a man who, on a deeper level, they know will be just as distant and unresponsive to their needs, they set up a ceaseless challenge of trying to capture the approval they never gained at home. To them, it is far better to establish that dynamic than analyze the real source of their pain—an intense dislike of themselves. So, in the beginning, when the man becomes abusive or tries to dominate her life, it is of course he who is at fault. She can complain about him (and that's not to say he doesn't share much of the responsibility; he certainly does). But Golden Handcuffs are the result of *two* insecure people, whose rendezvous in marriage brings out all their vulnerabilities. Some women will look most studiously for weak men, just so they can feel needed all the time; so they can get the constant validation they never received in adolescence. But most choose the man who they think will take care of them.

When things go bad and women get tired of blaming men, they come back to blaming themselves. After all, it *was* their fault that Daddy molested them, or spent no time with them. Therefore, it must be their fault that the once-lovable husband has turned into a demanding, inconsiderate stranger. The solution, they decide, is not to unlock the handcuffs, but rather to tighten them even further. Many of them have reached their late thirties, and as their looks have begun to fade—they feel that their grasp on their man, and thus on economic security, has weakened as well. Compounding this kind of person's insecurity is the persistent fear that another woman (the same model, but with much less mileage) could take her place on any given day. She's even *seen* that woman, who still is only in her twenties yet also wants the good life and is willing to do almost anything to get it. So the older women try to please their husbands even more, hoping that will be enough to keep them in line. They realize that their men may find their mothers once again in the younger women.

Women in the more affluent financial brackets demonstrate their dissatisfaction by seeking even greater materialistic comfort: "Okay, so maybe Andy *was* horrible to me today. Maybe I'm *not* getting the emotional support I need. I can live with that! I'll just take my Visa card to Bullocks, and pick up a few nice dresses and hats, and that'll make me feel better. If I have more things, then I really will be okay." And, for a while at least, it usually works. In fact, often these women are actually encouraged on such shopping trips by their spouses. Typically, the man will verbally abuse his wife, and then try to make up. "We had the worst fight in the world the other night," Leona told me during one especially painful visit. "John threw some of my dresses out the window, and broke the heels on my shoes. The next morning he came over to me and kissed me, as if nothing happened. He grabbed my hand, and suddenly there's a check in it. I couldn't believe it. It was for $5,000. I was happy to replace my things, but I really felt cheap when he handed me the money. He can buy me."

But shopping binges (like other kinds) are far from a cure; often they are like a drug high that wears off after only a few hours. Then the deep pain of loneliness and emptiness comes back with a vengeance. And *no* amount of trips to the mall (or whatever) will fill up *that* void. A lot of times these seemingly compulsive shoppers buy things because that is their only way of getting back at their husbands. "If I can damage his wallet, I can hurt him."

Other women choose to bury their shame in romance novels; they are literally addicted to that stuff. Imagery is the only way they can get through each day. They are hooked by the premise of being saved. Someday, they believe, it will happen to them; they will be saved from this horrible man. The problem is that the concept of a savior is what got them in trouble in the first place, and the longer they trust their future to a fantasy, a romance novel, the longer it will be before they take the steps necessary to change what's going on in real life. There are no Prince Charmings; everyone is flawed, and *they* must save *themselves*. Unfortunately, waiting each day for the fantasy to materialize severely increases the prognosis for a deep depression.

It is understandably difficult for these women to admit

their disappointment. So many have come into my office pretending that they are content in marriage—that we should stick to dealing with their chronic physical pain, or anxiety disorders. If they have any complaints against their husbands, they'll make excuses for them: "He didn't know what he was saying." All that does is allow the woman to avoid confronting him, and lets him off the hook.

When I ask if they are happy, they usually give some nebulous response such as "I guess so. I'm not sure whether anyone is really happy." When I ask them to define what "happy" would mean to them using specific terms, their heads will lower, and their sad, empty eyes will reveal the truth. It is like opening up a dam of tears, which they soon think will never stop flowing. The truth is even *worse* than they imagined, and they don't know what to do to make things better.

Now they're stuck. When they were living in their delusions, the pain was there, but they didn't have to identify it. As long as they ignored talking to themselves about the pain, they didn't have to bear the responsibility of carrying that knowledge around all the time, and therefore did very little to try to change the situation. They were experts in avoiding confrontation, simply so they wouldn't have to make a decision: Do I stay, do I demand change in this relationship or do I leave him? In their minds, any of these choices means they lose!

But, after verbalizing the problem, it's very difficult to go back. They will never be ignorant again. That *still* doesn't mean, however, that they've sworn to equalize the balance of power in their marriage. Many conclude that such an attempt would be too risky, and therefore that it is better to suffer in comfort than in poverty: "I'd rather be sad and lonely and have the things I need or want," Kimberly told me, "and be able to go to Bermuda twice a year, than try to start all over again." They are committing emotional suicide to maintain the Golden Handcuffs. Gloria, another victim sadly resigned to the status quo, told me, "I am no better than a whore. The only difference between me and a hooker is that she takes her $500 and leaves in the morning. I stay, day after day after day."

There are other fears, too. For example, if women who have children threaten to leave the marriage, their husbands will not stand for it. "Go ahead," the man will say, "but the kids aren't going with you. I've got the attorneys and the money, and you've got nothing." And, even if the women think they'll get to keep the kids, their nurturing instincts want to protect the children from the lingering trauma of a divorce. That is simply too much guilt for them to bear. Women will also contend that breaking up the marriage will forever isolate them from all the social contacts they've spent years building up. Yet another popular justification for hanging on is that they fear they won't be able to survive in the world without a man—a myth that popular culture has done little to dispel over the years. Or they might claim, "In two years, when the kids are gone, I'll deal with it," or "As soon as I feel physically stronger, I'll make my move."

All of these so-called defenses are merely excuses, an elaborate cover-up for the *real* reason they don't try to leave: When they finally leave, they are afraid of facing themselves, of taking a deep look at how extensively self-hatred has taken over their lives. Such an examination would reveal a pattern developed since childhood, and so sometimes they embark on an aimless journey from man to man, looking for diversions from their pain. Ultimately, none of the excuses stand up to scrutiny. The time comes when taking a stand is the choice. As in most situations, there are only a few choices: Do I stay? Do I confront and hang in there till positive changes occur? Do I leave?

To their credit, many women do try to make significant changes. They will attempt to gain more power in the relationship, whether it means looking for a job or demanding more knowledge of their economic status. Some women will also begin to lose weight—although, ironically enough, as much as the men want these particular trophies to be displayable at a moment's notice, they don't want their wives to look *too* good. So they often will sabotage any effort by the woman to gain greater control. "We don't have the money for you to do your hair," one man said. Sure, they had the money. He was just threatened by the thought that if his wife took charge, she might leave him. *She* might be the one to find a better model.

That's why a lot of men also don't want their wives to work. Such a situation would put them in the company of other men, and their insecurities couldn't tolerate that. "Brian could never believe that I would marry him," Michelle told me. "He always thought he wasn't good enough for me." In reality, Brian's shock over his good fortune never really went away; *that's* why he needed to control Michelle. If she started to accumulate more power, why would she need Brian anymore?

Many times, these women want *me* to put the handcuffs on them! They're willing to expend the tireless effort required to break away from their husbands, but not to live completely free of someone else's control. Naturally, I refuse to play that role. I am a coach, not their next guardian. Sometimes they don't respond well to that news, but as time goes on, they finally begin to embrace their emerging independence—a giant step toward a new, happier life.

Over the years, I have approached these women with the following goals:

- To make them understand the cycle of self-hatred that they have needlessly endured
- To show them how to accept themselves and realize that they haven't been fully responsible for their misfortune
- To help them bury a past they can't change
- To point out the undeniable rights they have as full human beings
- To help them make the necessary changes in their relationships with men
- To show them how to muster the courage to break away if their needs aren't met
- To explain to them that they are the ones who must repair the damage. They are the ones without power in the relationship. The person in control will never be the one to *voluntarily* share power.

In most cases we are talking about very intelligent women. Michelle was offered a scholarship to Smith College, but her father told her that further schooling was superfluous. "Michelle, you're cute," he told her—many more than just a few times. "Don't worry about it. A man will take care of you." Like so many other women, she grew up believing that she needed a man to make her "complete." Instead of realizing that she could dictate her future, she mistakenly assumed that somebody else should make the decisions. But now, as a new generation of women have grown up realizing a whole range of opportunities that in general were never before available to their sex, the pressure to avoid dependency has increased. Society says that they should be working, too—so they look at their situation, and it doesn't add up to the norm. They really do want to take the Golden Handcuffs off, and make a new life for themselves. But their men, always resistant to change, stand firmly in the way. Or do they continue to *allow* the perception of the man being in their way?

These women must learn to trust their intuition. On one or another level they knew early on that the men they were marrying were not really Prince Charmings. They each had an inkling of the future in that moment of clarity, not long into the relationship, when (for example) their lover said something abusive, or made a demand that wasn't fair. Yet this discovery was too painful to deal with right then, and they quickly decided it really hadn't happened—that it mirrored a side of him that didn't exist. It's amazing what people will do to avoid the truth. Over the years, they may even realize that their husband *isn't* (or *wasn't*) the worst man on earth. But they put him on such a lofty pedestal, subjecting themselves to such an inferior position, that when change inevitably occurs, it's that much more difficult to watch.

What's important for these women is that they saw these changes. They never lost their uncanny intuition; they just chose to ignore it as part of the deal they made to gain security. They will then admit how intuitive they really are, even if they've made unwise decisions. Opening up in therapy seems to help them realize they have merely placed their intuitive powers in storage and to realize that they have the ability to bring them back, a major step toward rebuilding their weakened self-esteem. There is no doubting that women have within them the power to unlock the Golden Handcuffs, but those in need of using it must mass the full courage of their convictions and then *act* on that. Many will say (of the cuffs), "I always figured that once I got into the relationship, I could take them off." But it takes more than words; it takes plenty of hard work.

These women must realize that, like alcoholics, they will never totally be rid of the problem. Because of their backgrounds, they will always be susceptible to entering another Golden Handcuffs relationship. That is why it is important to be fully aware of all the warning signals. I have counseled women who have felt the courage to leave numerous times when these symptoms cropped up, but instead, almost automatically, drifted into the next equally unacceptable relationship. It is the *pattern* that they must recognize. Unfortunately, some don't see it until the same behavior is replicated in their daughter's life. They will get angry and tell her to be more assertive with her boyfriend or husband—and only then, suddenly, they will understand where the objectionable behavior came from.

The work in this area is not easy. (If it were, I wouldn't have felt the need to write this book.) Yet most assuredly the changes can take place—and the rewards won't take forever. Fortunately, many women already have accepted the challenge and dramatically improved their lives. They have summoned their demons from the dungeons of their subconscious, and rendered them relatively harmless. They have taken the handcuffs off, and become free.

Kate was another patient who ostensibly came to see me about chronic pain, but quick to get to the real point of her visit. At thirty-eight and extremely attractive, she had been married for fifteen years, yet only the first fifteen months or so were even remotely satisfying. All the possessions of her life, the object of envy by so many of her friends, were not what they appeared to be—and, like so many others, she didn't know how to escape. Between tears, Kate told me:

"I've got everything I've always wanted. It's everything that my mother always wanted. I live in a beautiful dream house, and we have three cars in the garage. I don't have to work, and I can get my kids anything they desire. I should be the most grateful woman in the world. I'm not. I feel so lonely, so empty."

CHAPTER TWO

Do You Wear the Golden Handcuffs?

For years, Cynthia was too terrified to confront Darryl. She feared that if she said anything even slightly critical, he would pack up and leave her forever. And being alone was not something she could ever tolerate again. So she did nothing—until her anger boiled up inside so intensely that she couldn't hold it in any longer. She exploded in a rage, such as Darryl had never seen. And it seemed to work. Then one day, after eight months of on and off therapy, Cynthia had an announcement for me.

"Everything's perfect now. We've had some good long talks, and I think he finally understands that I deserve to be an equal partner in the relationship. When I told him that I may

seek a divorce because I felt that he had all the power and never heard what I said, he apologized and vowed to change. Last week, he showed me all of our financial records on the computer, and I was glad that he trusted me with this information. I feel that the handcuffs have finally come off. Dr. Olshan, I don't think I need to see you anymore."

But I knew better; I had seen this act before. Cynthia was like so many other women caught in the Golden Handcuffs, hesitant to make real change, more willing to live with the hell that was familiar than the unknown. Instead of challenging her too much, which would only have built up her defenses, I calmly asked her a few questions. "Just a wrap-up," I assured her; and she agreed.

"What have you learned about yourself?"

"I have learned how to like myself, how to realize that I deserve respect and happiness, and not to be treated like a second-class citizen."

"Where do you see the relationship going?"

"I see it becoming what it was supposed to become in the beginning. I see all the promises of the early days of our marriage coming true, after all. I see Darryl becoming the compassionate, nurturing man I thought I had married."

"How are you going to grow from here on?"

"I hope to go back to college and get my degree in speech communications, and maybe teach someday. I think Darryl would be receptive to that. He knows it's my time."

Cynthia is forty-six—her "time" was twenty years ago!

This case was not going to be easy to crack, yet I knew I had to unmask Cynthia's charade. Because if I let her go out of my office believing in her superbly-crafted web of illusion,

she might never again get this close to unlocking the handcuffs. So many women work hard to get to that point where
they can make a real difference, and then the dangers of
change become too intimidating and they return to their
former subservient roles. I had seen it so many times that it
made me sick to think of it. I had to stop Cynthia from
repeating this destructive pattern.

More questions:

"Who is going to pay for this school?"

"Darryl said he will, if we have the money."

"What do you mean 'if?' Before, you've told me that
there was plenty of money. He certainly had enough money
for his golfing trip to Florida. He certainly had enough
money for his poker games with the boys."

*"That was before. We're a little tight now, and I can't pay
for it with my allowance."*

"Your allowance? I thought you weren't getting an allowance any longer."

Cynthia froze. There were a few moments of silence. She
said, "Nothing's really changed, has it?" That was it: Disclos-
ing the allowance issue finally stopped her in the lie. Cynthia
had *no* money of her own. Like Michelle, every time she
wanted to buy a new slip, or even a soda, she had to seek
permission from her husband—who came home from work,
sat, delivered edicts to the family, and had his comforts
attended to by his wife. This requirement for permission had
been the case since the early days of their marriage in the
mid-1970s, and this was the one fact that, despite all of her
apparent progress, had not changed, and was not ever likely
to be different.

She curled up in her chair, almost in a fetal position, and couldn't look me in the face. She was angry at me because her delusion had been exposed. She was relieved, too: The truth takes so much less effort. When she walked out of the office she could only turn and say, albeit emphatically, *"See you next week."*

Following my own professional convictions, I had no interest in keeping Cynthia as a perpetual patient. Many therapists maintain a regular clientele for years, sometimes decades, but the truth is that in all too many cases very little progress is made nevertheless. People often waste an incredible amount of precious time (and hard-to-get money) immersing themselves in a past they cannot change, and failing to come to terms with a present wherein they can have much more power and control. Surely I wanted to see Cynthia move on—but not until I sincerely felt she was ready to take the handcuffs off.

Living in denial is, of course, nothing new or unique. *Everybody* plays this game from time to time. But the women in the Golden Handcuffs have become experts, frequently relying on it to spare themselves the fears we have already mentioned. So, obviously, the first and most important step toward changing your life has got to be the admission to yourself that you have a problem that needs to be addressed. This doesn't mean, however, that everyone suffers the problem to the same degree, or that each solution will provide the same results for each woman. But there are a number of common characteristics that usually indicate that financial imprisonment *has* taken place. Check the list below and see how many apply to you.

- The men in your life make the decisions on all the finances.
- You have difficulty being assertive.
- You tend to accept the blame for mistakes made by men in your life.
- As a child, you were denied approval by your parents—especially your father.
- You are afraid of being alone.
- You don't feel you deserve the happiness you think others have.
- You're vulnerable to stress disorders, such as headaches, ulcers, irregular menstrual cycles, and allergies.
- You measure success via a financial balance sheet.
- You are constantly comparing your possessions with those of other women.
- You feel that manipulation, deceit, and lying are justified for your financial gain.
- You look down on women with "traditional values."
- You are very insecure, and physical beauty is your obsessive quest.

If all (or even most) of these statements ring true, then it is safe to assume you *are* trapped in a Golden Handcuffs situation. Once you have admitted that you are—which is no small step—then you can begin figuring out ways to overcome the imbalance. But first there are a few fundamental rights that every woman should declare before tackling the pattern (which incidentally usually dates back to her childhood). These rights should be written down, and verbally repeated over and over, until you realize that they are crucial to your evolution as a woman of self-respect and dignity.

They are, in a sense, your Constitution, your mandate to change your life. At stake is nothing less than your survival.
You have the right to:

- Maintain your physical and emotional well-being.
- Seek help from others.
- Show negative feelings without guilt.
- Reject any attempt by the men in your life to manipulate you.
- Take pride in what you are accomplishing.
- Communicate honestly.

In short, you have the right to be happy and fulfilled, even if this means that the man you've been with can't come along with you. If he tries to deny these rights to you, which many do, it is not *your* responsibility to exhaust yourself trying to change *him*. Rather, it is *his* responsibility to recognize that you have equal rights within the relationship, that the two of you have the responsibility to compromise.

Many women who come to see me complain that the men in their lives will never change; that their age-old habits of control and manipulation have become a part of who and what they are. And that could very well be true: these men *may* never change. But I cannot work with those who see no need for change, even when life could be better. Usually, it is the women who evaluate their relationships and want them to improve. And there's no doubt that *they* can learn how to change. By trying to blame men for their inflexibility, the women are looking for yet another way to avoid confrontation—to keep themselves from examining their past and making peace with it. The key to unlocking the handcuffs is to realize that the women have always had the capacity. Now they must use it.

No one can change the past. Learning to accept both good and bad memories is essential to self-knowledge and self-esteem. Many women trapped in the Golden Handcuffs are victims of devastating childhood traumas, including incest, sexual molestation, and physical and psychological abuse. Some have merely "learned" to wear the handcuffs from their mother's behavior.

Although the past cannot be changed, it should not be used as an excuse for not taking action. Therapists are available and can help one work through these traumas. Sometimes we wait ten or even thirty years to finally release the ghosts that haunt our present relationships. Traumas of abuse are never resolved by pretending they never happened. Each woman must learn to understand how their past relationships with fathers, stepfathers, and other males and females may have helped them wear the Golden Handcuffs.

In resolving the past, which should be done as quickly as possible, it is important to take inventory and not to omit any of the major traumas. Otherwise, some of these hidden memories are likely to pop up over and over, sabotaging even the most courageous woman's efforts to make substantial progress. Once all of the alleged demons are exorcized (they are usually not quite as dangerous as first feared), you can switch your attention to the more important priority: the future.

The road to recovery is, of course, paved with many potholes, and so women must learn to navigate it carefully. Likewise, nobody is expected to alter lifelong patterns overnight. Many of these habits took decades to form, and aren't going to give up their dominant status without a major fight. Because, as much as the women who come to see me want to break away from the handcuffs, many of them will struggle desperately to maintain the status quo. What happens, therefore, is that when the first major changes are attempted, the women experience a tremendous sense of anxiety.

Unfortunately, many women will give up when anxieties first appear, and that is quite understandable. They are looking for the most immediate way to find some kind of peace again, and abandoning the new changes is the easiest approach to accomplishing that. But, as I try to tell them, all this move does is grant a temporary reprieve from the *real* source of their emotional pain. Almost instantly, that uneasiness will reemerge, and the desire to fix it will, of course, follow again. They must understand that these kinds of anxiety reactions are quite normal—many others have them. But no important changes can happen without anxiety. It's similar to the kind of helpful nervousness one feels before giving a speech or taking a big test.

Maintaining their present behavior is a dead end. They will argue that their husband is the one who is causing their anxiety. Not quite. It is the women who are letting themselves become anxious—and once they see that they can be in control of neutralizing these reactions, they gain their first sense of power in dealing with the relationship. If they can control their own internal behavior, then they can control how they act toward their husbands. They can see that the worst that can happen is that the man *won't* adapt to their needs, but that they *will* remain strong and intact, anyway.

Many women seem to have difficulty admitting that they deserve to have rights. I can't tell you how many times I've heard women come into my office and be shocked to hear that they, too, deserve the same general privileges normally afforded a man. It may, in fact, be the first time in their lives that someone has told them that they *have* rights. I will ask them to read the list, and they will oblige—but it will sound as if they're reading the rights that apply to other women, not them. One woman said to me, "There must be a mistake. Those are a man's rights." No, they are a woman's rights, too.

Some will look at women who exercise their rights, and try to demean them: "Well, she's a real bitch, anyway," or "She has a good reason because of what he has done to her," or "She doesn't know how good she had it before she became a feminist." Stop. We are not talking about feminism here. We are talking about a woman's prerogative to be treated in the same fair and decent way that men expect for themselves. These women are trying to justify their inability to believe in their own rights, when in reality there is no justification for perceiving themselves as second-class citizens.

Those men who are anxious to keep their supremacy, who manipulate rights to their advantage, will say things such as "I think a woman should always come first because she has the responsibility of bearing children," or "Of course you have rights, honey." But in most cases these men are merely paying lip service to the *assertion* of their wife's independence. If the wife believes he will grant those rights, she will stay—and he will continue to control her. The so-called Prince Charming, the man who has arrived to rescue the maiden in distress, is often the first man to affirm her rights. She hears that, and she is hooked for good.

The foundation for the Golden Handcuffs is money, and by initiating a pattern of lavish gifts, a man can start the woman on a trail of dependency that is both very tempting and damaging. And it may be years before she even thinks about trying to break free. "I'll take care of everything," he'll say. "You just relax and let me worry about it." Who wouldn't jump at that kind of protection? Once again, let me clarify that there is *nothing wrong* with giving or accepting gifts as long as they don't have an undisclosed price tag of control. In other words, motive is everything.

The bait works at an emotional level, too: Prince Charming often zeroes in on a woman who is especially vulnerable after the breakup of her most recent relationship. "How could he have done that to you?" he asks. "I care about you and I understand. *I* will be different from any other man you have met." A woman in pain will hear that and feel she is being saved. Some of these men are so adroit at utilizing the bait technique that they make professional con men pale by comparison.

It will never be easy for women to resist this kind of manipulation. For that matter, it's not easy for anyone to resist the charm of someone who "understands" them and is dedicated to this happening. Underneath it all, of course, is the fear of confronting the truth about themselves—the trail of self-blame and self-loathing that extends far beyond any objective analysis. But that fear is played out in many forms, including the anxieties they have about their financial status and the specter of singlehood. And as long as they are with men, even the most domineering ones, they don't have to deal directly with this hidden reality. They may spend their time furious with their husbands, but they feel it is better than a life alone.

This simply doesn't have to be the case. It is important

for these women to understand that it really is okay to be alone, and many people are, even within the context of a relationship. Jennifer is a typical example of this conundrum. She compromises all the time, sacrificing her own needs to please her husband. She is forty-two now, a singer who stopped singing, a woman once intent on conquering the world but one who has become afraid of leaving her home. Everything has become a distraction from her goals.

"We do the things constantly that Adam wants to do. He likes the ballpark, and I like the museum. We've seen the Dodgers eight times this year; we've been to the museum once. When he leaves for work in the morning, I immediately turn on "Donahue" and watch soap after soap. If I have to go to the grocery store, I make sure it's a quick trip, and I come right home. It makes me feel uneasy to be alone for any length of time without a chore, without doing something for Adam. That's just the way things are around here."

Jennifer, like so many other women, is terrified of being alone. So, instead, she will surrender to the handcuffs and demean herself, day after day, to avoid the alternative. Such women equate being alone with failure. The cause is probably societal and a carry-over from almost every culture that says a woman must have a man to take care of her.

Society still doesn't help matters. Being alone has a horrible social connotation, especially for a woman. A man dines alone at a nice restaurant, and nobody gives him a second thought, but the same is not so for a woman. See a woman by herself at the movies, and there must be something wrong with her. One of the ways for a woman to unlock the handcuffs is to learn *how* to be alone. She has to say, "I choose to be alone. I will choose *when* I want to be alone."

Women can conquer this fear—and learn that solitude, in addition to possessing a natural soul-cleansing effect, can open the mind to great self-discovery and amusement. Instead of being afraid to be alone, a woman should learn how to treasure solo time—including taking a mental inventory of everything in life, and especially in her marriage.

What I typically suggest to many women patients is that they begin the process of being alone through careful, well-managed increments. They first learn to be alone for a specific period of time (initially not more than an hour or so), and they should have in mind a specific purpose in being alone. Watching television, or even reading a book, doesn't count because that really isn't being alone—it is being by yourself with a distraction, yet another tool to keep you away from your deepest thoughts, from understanding more about what you want and deserve in life, from understanding what you want in a relationship and how your needs can be met. (Once again, I'm going to emphasize, only you can determine *your* needs, and after they have been established, only then can you negotiate with your significant other to establish joint needs.)

First establish an atmosphere that is conducive to introspection. I regularly advise women to take leisurely walks through the neighborhood, or sit in a park with their thoughts. Initially, at least, this routine will be extremely discomforting for most women. For example, they will experience severe anxiety reactions, mostly associated with guilt. The first temptation will be to jump back in the car and rush home, even if their husband is at work. Primarily, they still are very apprehensive about connecting with themselves.

Women who are afraid to be alone really don't like themselves.

Again, I tell these women not to give in to their feelings of anxiety; that if they hurry back home all they are doing is subjecting themselves to more of the same general unhappiness that caused them to see me in the first place. Often I must point out to them the costs of reducing that anxiety by taking the quick way out: You will again feel diminished. You will again feel that you have given up control of *your* life. You will again feel as if you'll never become the woman you were meant to be. You will never remove the handcuffs. Thankfully, when that is understood, many choose to endure the anxiety. No pain, no gain!

After practice time and the acceptance of self, the women learn that they have power they had never imagined. By defying the anxieties that could have caused them to give up on their quest for self-respect, they will usually not revert to the powerful hold of the Golden Handcuffs. By learning to be alone, and even to be happy thereby, they start to like themselves more and more, and realize that they needn't diminish themselves to be acceptable to a man. If a man is going to win their favor, he's going to have to deal with the whole package, not with some poorer facsimile created by a woman's deep vulnerabilities.

Linda proved the point. When she first came to see me in 1987, she was a wreck. I tried to get her to experiment with being alone, and the results were disastrous.

"Dr. Olshan, I can't do it. I sit there, and I start to break out in a sweat, and I don't know why. It's a beautiful day, and I just go for a simple walk in the neighborhood. But then, my

whole body starts to shake, and I hurry back home. I close the door, get a drink, and begin to calm down. I can't keep going on those walks."

But Linda did return to those walks, because she knew that life with Jerry wasn't going to get better until she confronted herself. Two months later, she told a very different story.

"Everything has changed. I look forward to being alone. It's like greeting an old friend you haven't seen in years, someone you really know better than anyone else. We have fun together. We realize how much we like each other, and really how mean we've been to each other over the years. It has helped my relationship with Jerry enormously. Will he be able to live with the new me, and not try to play the emperor any more? I don't know, and frankly, I'm not as worried about it as I used to be. That's because I know that I'll survive whatever happens in my marriage. I know I will be the same person with or without Jerry."

Linda eventually *did* leave Jerry, and started a new life. She dates frequently, and from what I can tell, none of the men sounds like a Prince Charming trying to save her. Linda doesn't need to be saved. She saved herself.

The fear of being alone is not the only pitfall for the women of the Golden Handcuffs Group. There are many other causes for their trepidation—for their reluctance to deal straightforwardly with the men whom they have granted the power to control a relationship. Prominent on that list, of course, is their fear of the streets. They've read stories about the women of the 1980s and 1990s, the so-called new poor who wind up in shelters. Or, even if they don't worry about total disaster, they certainly can't imagine life without many of the comforts to which they are accustomed.

Candice, who qualified for the latter category, found herself in a constant internal war. She had to change something in her marriage to Dan, but she clearly wasn't willing to pay the price.

"How can I give up this life? I don't want to live like my parents did, scraping from paycheck to paycheck, scared to death that something unexpected would happen each month to throw off the budget. It was horrible. I never had the things other kids got, and I blamed them for it. Well, my kids get what they want, and so do I. My credit card practically has no limit, and that's the way I like it. I know that Dan sees me as his possession, and I know I am completely at his mercy for each handout. But without money, I'd be completely at the mercy of the world out there, and that's not for me."

Candice's confession deeply disturbed me. In a way, she made perfect sense, and I could feel her desperation over entering a new life without the privileges she now enjoyed. But I also knew that she was hanging on to that security at the expense of her pride and self-esteem. That's a very steep price to pay.

When Candice came back, it was an opportunity for me to be totally blunt. I pointed out that things with Dan probably were *never* going to get better. In fact, if anything, they were going to get much worse. Because of his insecurities, he could continue to seize power at every chance, making her life miserable.

Typically, women who face the loss of self-esteem that comes with domination by another may decide that the way to improve their life is to do *more* things for their man. The mentality is: If I make his life better by doing more for *him*, then he will be happier, and then he will treat me better and ultimately want to make me happy.

That is a twisted psychology, but it is what drives many of the women in Golden Handcuffs. They don't think of what their men can do to make them better satisfied, and what they can do for themselves that will improve the circumstances. They think that if they're good little girls, as they were with Daddy, the reward will come. They're always filled with excuses for their man: If his *boss* treats him better at work, everything will be better with *us*. If his *mother* doesn't complain to him anymore, he'll treat *me* better. And so on.

Doing more comes in a variety of forms. Many women will try to give the man more sex, better sex, or both—whatever he wants. Or they'll spend hours and hours in the kitchen, putting together the perfect meal. They've made subservience into an art form, and are turning over control of their future to someone else.

Let me clarify a significant point. There are many people who do all of the above out of reciprocal love, not fear. There is a great difference when the motive is mutual love rather than submission. It is important to refrain from constantly defending your husband. No matter what concessions you may get from him, the simple truth is that you will travel a very difficult road to gain equal financial status. The women become frightened—and I have seen some of them slump so far down in their chairs that they seem to get smaller and smaller. Many women continue (or at least begin) to fantasize about other men. It is important that these women understand that their self-esteem is diminishing significantly and that there is an urgency for change. It's a self-portrait that is hard to paint, and even harder to have to stare at.

Candice was a very frightened woman who needed to evaluate her talents and determine what she could do to gain economic independence either within or out of her relationship. What were her skills? Her career options?

Too many women give in to their husband's treats and never consult an attorney themselves to discover what their rights truly are. Knowledge of your legal rights and a valid assessment of your talents can give you a realistic evaluation of where your life has the potential to go.

It is important to be pro-active and discover the difference between truths and threats. When this is done, you will be less likely to feel constantly ashamed or wonder if life can ever be different. You will be less likely to feel that you have to indulge yourself in the fantasy of a romance novel because "that's the only escape." And, hopefully, you will not feel that whatever you do for your man is not enough. Instead, you can feel, for the first time in years, like a full human being, full of pride and dignity. You can feel like life has started over. Life can become stimulating if you demonstrate the courage to face the challenge and the willingness to watch for change.

CHAPTER THREE

The Rationalization Game

One big trap in relationships is the traditional tendency of the woman to blindly agree to whatever the man wants. She becomes a slave to his every whim, unable to assert her own desires and opinions, as if these didn't matter. While this pattern may upset her, and even cause deep resentment, more than likely she will do little to alter the status quo. The reason once again is clear: fear.

Women say yes to whatever a man desires because they are afraid that saying no will spark a confrontation—and a confrontation is the last thing these women want. A confrontation means that they must come to terms with the full extent of their dissatisfaction, and, once that is acknowledged, it might be necessary to make a decision: Do I stay or do I go? Either way, the answer is very unpleasant.

Of course, these women try valiantly to play the game of rationalization: "If *I* say yes, that means that on another occasion *he* will say yes. Likewise, if I say yes, that means I will begin building up an impressive backlog of compliance which will finally give me some power in the relationship." The woman begins to replay her former role as the daughter always searching for her father's love. Then, it was: "If I say yes, Daddy will buy me an ice cream cone. And if I do my homework and get A's in school, Daddy will love me and pay attention to me." But the truth was that Daddy may have been too self-centered to be the man you hoped he could be.

This thinking is completely twisted. Once again, these women aren't thinking about what they can do to fill themselves up; they are looking for someone else to do the job for them. They are relying on another person to validate them, and they assume that the way to accomplish this is to say yes to every request. Besides the fact that they become far too dependent on another person's whims, the simple truth is that they will *never* fill themselves up this way. It all results only in the same kind of disappointment that they have experienced since childhood. As children, we learn to appreciate ourselves because we receive positive validation, which reinforces our worth. If we don't receive this, we experience a growth process saturated with disappointment following disappointment.

Each time a woman says yes to what *he* wants, especially when it runs counter to her intrinsic desires, she is feeding his need for control. She is admitting that *he* runs the relationship. In fact, he may not care so much about the activity as he

does about making sure the woman remains firmly under his domination. And, by not asserting herself, she enforces his notion that she deserves little respect. He starts to think that any woman so unwilling to fight for her wishes *should* be treated this way.

In some cases the woman becomes convinced that the man is *right* to deny her desires. I had a woman come to see me who had kept trying to convince her husband to let her go to the movies with her girlfriends. (That's right, *let* her go.) After months of getting nowhere with him on that matter, this woman finally "realized that he did the right thing" in refusing to grant his permission. "I should be home when he's around," she told me. "I see what he means." What she didn't seem to see was that it was not her prerogative to question the fact that he went bowling on Tuesday night, played poker on Friday, and golfed on Sunday afternoon! That was okay, though, because he was a working man who needed to relax with "the guys."

Many women who are caught in the Golden Handcuffs have difficulty saying no to men whom they seem to place in positions of authority. They may have developed this view of men through their mother's role-modeling, which made the father an absolute authority figure in the household. So there is a real dichotomy in their perception because they grew up watching their mother verbalize their belief in the father's authority and yet manipulate him to try to "win" against it. What this teaches a young woman is that the approach of expressing honest or assertive feelings is unacceptable and that an indirect approach of manipulation is the only alternative.

The inability to say no carries a very expensive price tag.

These women grow up to be pleasers, always afraid that saying no or taking a stand for their beliefs will result in rejection by men. They suffer from the lack of independent thinking in their relationships involving any men whom they perceive to be in authority—including their father, husband, boss, or even their doctor.

Unfortunately, for some women sexual relationships with a man become one of the areas in which they are afraid to say no for fear of rejection. The inability to be assertive and make independent sexual decisions can have lifelong consequences. Nancy, a former patient of mine, is a revealing example of women who have difficulty saying no to male authority figures. Nancy believes that if she refuses to abide by a man's request for sex, he will reject her. Yet each time she does say yes out of fear, she feels an equally unsettling sensation of self-loathing. Nancy's Golden Handcuffs were in great measure held tight by her misconception that men should always be in authority, and this included the men she dated. Her mother's relationship with her father had long ago etched the pattern that Nancy was imitating. Nancy had come to the realization that she needed help.

Months went by, and her progress was minimal. Nancy would leave my office full of energy and confidence, then call me the next day, full of sorrow and regret. Then, at long last, she finally told me about what she considered the biggest triumph of her therapy.

"I said no to a man last night for the first time. I never thought it would happen. He wanted to stay the night, but I told him no. He kept asking, maybe five or six times, before I almost had to push him out the door. It felt great to say no."

But Nancy, I quickly found out, had told me only part of

the story. It seems that while she did say no to him about spending the night, she had already made love to him several times, even though she was ostensibly totally opposed to the idea. *"He kept pushing and pushing. What was I supposed to do? I couldn't say no to that. It was horrible."*

At first glance it appears Nancy was still in the same weak position as when she started: A man wanted to sleep with her, and she couldn't refuse, but I prefer to see things another way. She had in fact (even if not quite in time) *said* no to a man, and that meant a lot. She at least was able to decide that she wasn't going to do *all* of what he wanted, and that was a start. I believed Nancy would progressively make bigger strides as she realized that saying no would not ruin her life. If anything, it would revitalize it. It was not long before Nancy's first tentative steps turned into full strides. By the end of therapy, she no longer felt the need to please and submit sexually based on misconceptions of rejection. Over time, she gained control of this aspect of her life and developed respect for her own wishes and desires. She finally considered herself someone worth caring about.

Learning how to say no will not be mastered overnight. It will demand a kind of intense scrutiny that most of these women have never faced and that requires plenty of practice. With persistence, it eventually can be controlled.

Practice saying no to people whose rejection will not directly affect your life. When you step into territory that will affect your life more directly, think before you speak. A common statement I hear is, "I didn't want to do it, but I was shocked when they asked me, so I said yes." Or, "I didn't feel exactly right about saying yes, but I couldn't think of a good excuse." What I'm about to say is very important regarding this issue. You don't have to give a response immediately. You have the right to take the time to think about how you feel. As you practice this, you will find that there will be a shorter timespan between what doesn't feel quite right but you don't know why, and your own understanding of your feelings. Practice saying, "I'll think about that and let you know later"—or in an hour or tomorrow. You pick the time to answer. It's your decision for commitment, your response!

The first question women must ask themselves is: Do I *really* want to do what he is asking? Whether it means going to the movies or having sex, women must stop to decide if the activity in question is something they are interested in pursuing. Instead of automatically saying yes, even when their intuition is heavily opposed to the proposal, this new habit, if adopted, will change everything. They will be taking the steps to put themselves on an equal level, learning how to be decision makers.

Another good way to learn how to give the response you feel good about is to ask the man to clarify his request instead of trying to read his mind. What this does is make the man repeat the questions and allow you time to avoid the pitfall of the automatic yes-or-no response and to give serious consideration to whether it's really about something that interests her or is in her best interest. In short, she is allowing herself a new way of making decisions by letting her long-repressed intuition do the work. She is learning how to become an independent thinker.

Naturally, as in all the other cases in which the woman seeks a balance of power in the relationship, the man losing control will fight back. No one, man or woman, gives up power easily or willingly. When she asks for clarification, she sends out a warning signal that things aren't as easy as they used to be. Expect negative reactions to this.

One "B" tactic of interfering with the new behavior is to hurry up the process, and perhaps thereby rattle the woman. If she becomes flustered she will likely abandon her new technique and return to her familiar subservient role. Men will say something like "Well, if you have to think about it that long, then forget it!" Or they might say, "You can't take *that* long for a decision. I won't have *time* to explain it more." And of course the man will hope the woman becomes angry—which is exactly what happens much of the time. Anger fully resurrects all of her anxiety, and she starts to repeat the cycle of indecision and thereby dependency.

Men are very *shrewd* when defending their territory. Sometimes they will frame a request in such a way that if a woman says no, she'll appear to be insulting her own intelligence. This tactic works especially well in front of other people: "Oh, honey, you're always so good at judging where we should go. Don't you think we all ought to eat Italian tonight?" The woman is in a trap. If she goes against his suggestion, she'll appear to be bucking the wishes of everyone. The man is after control, and the woman at first feels flattered until she realizes she has been manipulated once again.

Inevitably, the woman will wind up in a position where she is justifying her response to a request. And he simply will not take no for an answer. One day, a patient named Catherine told me about a conversation she had with her husband, Hal. Hal loved sports and, as usual, wanted to take her to a ball game. Catherine, as usual, didn't want to go. This was always the scenario, and always they went. But after therapy, Catherine was ready to make a stand.

"I can't go to the game," she told Hal.

"Why not? You always go, and you have a good time. Come on."

"I don't really feel that well."

Hal *had* to accept her answer, and suddenly it seemed that Catherine had triumphed—she had learned how to say the magic word and make it work.

Not exactly: Catherine was lying. She felt fine; she *just didn't want to go* to the game. So, instead of confronting Hal with the truth, she resorted to a falsehood in order to get what she wanted. But deception is not good enough. Women who rely on it to outmaneuver their men are not really liberating themselves from the Golden Handcuffs. All they are doing is buying time—*and* anxiety, because each lie makes them resent the fact that they didn't feel strong enough to tell the truth. And the price they pay for that is much greater than any confrontation, no matter how ugly.

Understandably, as I have said before, this new role will not be an easy one for women. Besides the personal baggage they carry, they must bear the weight of social opinion. Society has told them that men can be aggressive and demanding, yet have the right to stick to their principles. Women, however, are expected to give in. These stereotypes *are* changing but not fast enough for the women in the Golden Handcuffs. They can't afford to wait that long. They must remember daily that they should enjoy the same fundamental rights as men.

Society also tells women not to criticize their men. So many women in relationships these days remember mothers who wouldn't dare say anything negative to or against their husbands. They stood by helplessly as their mothers refused to stand up for their rights. If they asked them why they didn't fight back, their mothers could only say "You don't understand."

Well, today it *is* the job of women to be honest when it is warranted. This is in fact a crucial issue for the women in the Golden Handcuffs: If *they* can verbalize *their* discontent with *their* men, then perhaps both sides will be able to iron out the key differences and salvage a good relationship. Fighting back is one of the most fundamental rights women have, because it strikes right at the core of their right to be happy and fulfilled.

There is both a proper and an improper way to apply criticism, but most women who are financially tied to their husbands or boyfriends usually choose the improper way: They don't go far enough. Karen is a perfect example. For almost three years, Karen had been furious with her husband's inability to recognize all the work she did at home. He never praised her, and had a comment only when she wasn't, in his view, doing something well enough. She finally summoned the courage to say something.

"Bill, I think you did a great job with the McIntosh case. Nobody thought you could get a settlement, but you did. I'm really proud of you. By the way, have you noticed I've done a lot lately to keep the house in good shape? You never say anything."

For Karen, that was a big step. But not *big* enough—

because, like so many other women, she didn't *say* enough to effect real change. By first complementing Bill, and refusing to vent the full depth of her anger, she failed to pass a message to him that might have altered his behavior. Her complaint plainly didn't register.

Many women tell me that their men don't hear them, don't listen to what they say. I believe that's probably because they don't give a direct message. If you want someone to understand you, don't leave room for them to second-guess what you are trying to say. Be firm!

Many times criticism is stated too quickly, as if the woman believed that merely uttering her point would get her somewhere. Again, all she's really trying to do is avoid confrontation, yet feel that she has been sticking by her principles. Here, too, the man isn't likely to change. He probably *still* won't respect what the woman has said—at least enough to give a positive response. It is extremely difficult to unlock the handcuffs until you can *firmly* stick by your principles.

One of the first rules to observe is to pick an appropriate time. Don't wait for halftime of the football game. Choose a time and a setting that will allow you the best opportunity to get your point across. It must be when there are no likely distractions that will allow a way to break away if things get a bit rough.

Women must be aware, of course, that men, if sufficiently threatened, will look for a way to gain (or regain) the advantage. Often they will try to force the issue right away, by asking the women to state (or restate) their case. Their purpose is to keep the women off balance, so that they can retain control of the relationship. A woman may say (for example) that she'd rather wait, because "I don't want to talk in front of the kids," and he'll likely respond, "Oh, that's okay." That's not good enough! Remember, choosing the turf and the ground rules enhances the woman's chances for success.

Raising issues during "Monday Night Football" (if your husband is a sports fan) may represent exceptionally bad timing. The man will have the opportunity to say, "Honey, the *game* is on. This really isn't a good time." The woman will be crushed: She has given him a back door, an out, a way to later claim that he didn't really catch what she was saying, because he wanted to watch the game. Some women will deliberately set up a situation like this merely because they don't want to confront issues. One reason for such nonconfrontational behavior is the past: these women grew up listening to their parents argue and so vowed never to repeat the performance. Confrontation is the last thing they want. When events seem headed in that direction, they do whatever they can to put a stop to it, even if that means once again sacrificing their dignity as women.

What must be remembered is that the confrontation will be easier to handle than the pain experienced in avoiding it. The anger, the frustration, the disappointment—they will all be there, whether they "say" something or not. And their children will sense this even though they may not verbalize it. So it's much better to make the point, get it on the record, and then try to get on with things. Only then can the pattern of standing up for one's rights be developed.

However, even if the time and place are appropriate, there is still the matter of putting the issue forward in a constructive manner. A woman must first carefully reason out what the exact issue is that bothers her, and then tell it to the man without launching an all-out assault on his character and decency or dredging up ages of past inequities. If the woman goes too far, for example, by bringing up points not central to the main issue, the man will feel that he is being *attacked*, and will certainly not be receptive. This will also hurt the woman, obviously, since she will have little chance to effect the desired change.

Annette, who in two years went from a shy, obedient pushover to a woman clutching her rights with amazing vigor, wasn't always skillful at confrontation. In one visit, she described how she used to go too far with her husband.

"Once I got started, I didn't know where to stop. I'd find myself thinking that I was mad at one thing, and then I'd be going off in another direction; this could happen three or four times in the same conversation. I couldn't stay focused on any one thing. The discussions became shouting matches, and nothing was accomplished."

They became shouting matches because Annette wasn't able to clearly state her one area of concern without sounding demeaning and didactic. Over the years, though, she learned how to approach her husband.

"I realized it was all a matter of telling him how I felt. If I made accusations and started to read his mind, the battle would be lost because he would then attack me, and I would attack him, and so on. It was only when I started to see that I had to concentrate on what I felt that any progress was achieved. If I told him that I felt he was being distant, or I felt hurt because I thought he was treating me poorly, it was difficult for him to argue. My feelings are my feelings, and he is not the judge of them."

Exactly! The way to criticize is to tell the man *how you feel*. Don't try to read his mind and interpret his intentions.

Even if you're psychic, that does no good. He will invariably deny your pronouncements, and the discussion will be lost. And don't dig up the past, rehashing old events and apparent transgressions that can't serve the discussion already under way. He will only resent that, as well; and it demeans the accuser, too. The women who have unlocked the handcuffs all have learned how to confront properly and effectively. That skill clearly is one of the building blocks for piecing together the assertiveness and courage to affirm one's rights, as well as for constructing a foundation on which to start a new life.

Learning how to *accept* criticism also is very important. For the women in the Golden Handcuffs, being criticized is their worst nightmare. It immediately conjures up all the old feelings relating to her relationship with her father. She felt she wasn't good enough then, and when her husband begins to air his grievances, she feels she isn't good enough now. She takes his complaints as the definition of her character: "He is upset with me, and therefore I must be bad. I must be wrong."

But none of that is true. If the man goes on the offensive, the woman should try as hard as possible to listen to the merits of his complaint, and not automatically perceive it as an indictment of her self. It might be difficult, perhaps almost impossible, but the way to respond is not to reintroduce old criticisms of her own, and thus revive past indiscretions, in trying to even the score. The key here is to deal with the issue up front, while maintaining dignity and asserting the *right* of the individual.

Often the most difficult emotion for women to express is anger—but unfortunately, for those burdened by the Golden Handcuffs, anger is usually precisely what they feel. These women were taught that anger isn't something they should demonstrate. If women express anger, they won't see themselves as the good little girls Daddy wanted them to be. So they'll talk to their friends, or let it out in passive–aggressive ways. Many actually think that if they merely *look* angry, that will be enough to get their point across. Not quite. What women need to do is *communicate* that anger—or else there's no chance that anything will ever change.

Dealing with criticism, whether giving it or receiving it, is only one facet of the most important element of changing the psychology behind the Golden Handcuffs. Later on, we will get to the specific financial rights that women have, and how to demand them. But that action should take place only after a lot of work is done at more fundamental levels. Women must first learn how to communicate with their men.

Of course, among each other, women can be experts at the process. It is widely believed that women are much more capable of honest, compassionate communication than men could ever dream of being. Women, among each other, can usually make their points without distortions, without compromises, without hiding their emotions. But for the women trapped by the Golden Handcuffs, that all changes when they talk to men. They turn into models of restraint, self-deception, fear. They hide more than they reveal, and then profoundly regret it. They rarely say what they really want to say.

Following are four patterns of communicating that are normally adopted by the women in the Golden Handcuffs:

Filtering: Taking the negatives the man tells her, and magnifying them, while filtering out all the positive aspects.

Here women are looking for ways to beat themselves up. This act confirms their perennial role as victim. Instead, a woman should take pride in the positive things a man communicates to her—while not, however, allowing those accolades to obscure any abusiveness or mistreatment that might occur. Because a man compliments a woman does not mean he has the right to deprive her of the equality she deserves. It doesn't mean that he has the right to make all the financial decisions.

Mind reading: Engaging in too much projection, instead of listening, women try to read a man's mind, imagining his motives and thoughts, and don't carefully attend to the words he says. Let's be careful, however, to remember that men in the Golden Handcuffs do have other motives, mostly tied to their desperate need for control. But, more importantly, the goal here is for women to improve their communication skills—and proper listening is one vital ingredient.

Blaming: Accepting responsibility for all the problems in communication: "If it's the wrong time, it's my fault. If he doesn't understand what I'm saying, it's my fault. If we argue, it's my fault." Well, guess what? Sometimes it *is* your fault, and sometimes it *isn't*. But whatever the case, what matters here is the tendency to assume that such breakdowns are always your fault. Women must learn that breakdowns simply are natural consequences of intense conversation, especially when emotionally explosive issues are at stake.

Justifying: Instead of relying on what they *feel*, women find themselves in the position of being asked to recall specific facts to back up their feelings, like a witness being interrogated. Men know just how to back women into that "nothing but the facts" corner. But what really matters is that this overt action by the man makes the woman feel uncomfortable, and this discomfort is what needs to be expressed, not justification for feelings. If women don't follow their feelings, then it's very likely they will allow themselves to be dragged into an argument that will prove unsatisfying.

To summarize some better ways to communicate, here are a few suggestions to keep in mind:

- Be specific when you voice your complaint.
- Ask for a reasonable change in his behavior.
- Stick to one issue at a time.
- Don't be sarcastic or intolerant.
- Always consider compromise.
- Don't allow counterdemands before the original demand is fully discussed.
- Don't predict how he will react.
- Don't assign labels to him.
- Take time to be sure of your real feelings.
- Learn how to hear what is being discussed. Don't allow old "childhood tapes" to influence the here and now of a relevant discussion.

Together, the thrust of these points is to clearly state your problem assertively, yet without vindictiveness, and explain the change of behavior that you desire. Maintain your dignity as a woman, and do not demean the man. Do not revert to name calling. Ideally, he will listen to your complaints and propose solutions. Of course, because his control is dissipating, he may not be very receptive—but that is another matter. The important thing is to state your case and go from there.

Glenda, forty-five, was married to Ken for eighteen years. They had three children, and a big house in the suburbs. To their friends, they were the ideal couple. But Glenda was an emotional wreck who, after several years of therapy, finally confronted Ken. It was not a pleasant scene.

"I was no longer a doormat. I told him time after time what things bothered me, and I didn't waver. After each conversation, I felt stronger. I felt that the individual I was meant to be was finally emerging from years of isolation. Frankly, I wasn't too concerned with how he would respond, although I did want to save our marriage. I was more concerned with saving myself, with preserving the spirit of independence that had been lost in all my years with Ken. When it started to come out, I felt a sense of liberation that I had never experienced. Ken, it turned out, couldn't deal with the new me, and I left him. But I've never been happier. The fear of a life without Ken was much worse than the reality. The reality is that I'm myself again."

Needless to say, perhaps, when women begin to employ these new communication techniques, they will, at first, feel extremely uncomfortable. The old, familiar anxieties will crop up again, and many women at this point will surrender, and return to their former ways. But they must persevere by accepting the anxieties and continuing to change. Only then will they evolve into the full human beings they were meant to be. Only then will they have a chance to be happy and fulfilled, hopefully still within their marriage.

Many times, the man will realize that the woman was right about something, and say, "The little woman may have a point here." It is a remarkably demeaning comment. It is as backhanded a compliment as one can receive. At times, men will also try to interrupt a request. That's another way to get the woman distracted from her game plan. The woman must make it clear that she doesn't appreciate being interrupted, and she wants to be heard, especially if he, in turn, wants her to listen to his point of view. "Let me finish my statement, and then you can state your point," she should say. At any rate, it is important not to allow the interruption to slow down momentum.

But men are not the only ones who try to sabotage the woman gaining power in the relationship. Believe it or not, other *women* will try to interfere. Jane, thirty-nine, finally realized that she could match up to the men in her social clique, but then found out that her female friends weren't comfortable with her new power.

"They started to exert pressure on me in the most subtle ways. I first noticed it when we were at a dinner party. The women took the dishes and went aside to chat. I've been through enough of those [chats] to know what they're all about. But this time, I was content to talk to the men, and it was great. They seemed a little weird about it, but I kept up on every level—politics, sports, whatever. But then one of the women called me into the kitchen. She told me she wanted to talk to me, but she really had nothing urgent to say. It was clear that she and the others were threatened by me talking to the men. Over the months, I found the women distancing them-selves from me. They couldn't take the new me."

They couldn't take the new Jane because the new Jane refused to accept second-class status. She could play with the big boys, and that terrified the other women. They saw that she had begun doing what they secretly wished they could do, but didn't have the courage. So, rather than witness the pain of their own failures, they desperately tried to bring Jane back into their fold. But for Jane it was too late, and they knew it. Jane had made the transition.

The women who learn how to communicate undergo amazing changes, both spiritually and physically. They start to use strong, declarative statements when talking to their husbands. Instead of framing things in a tentative, questioning style, they boldly make their points. They aren't waiting to be knighted by the king. Women who make these changes even begin to walk differently; and they actually look taller. Their new confidence spreads to all other facets of their life, too, both personally and professionally. They have discovered how to be complete human beings.

So far, we've dealt with some of the fears shared by women in the Golden Handcuffs and how they might overcome them. We've discussed how important it is to learn how to be alone, to learn that it is okay to confront issues. These changes are at the root of starting a new life—but now it's time to come up with specific solutions for dealing with the complicated *financial* problems that invade these relationships.

Women must learn how to use their new assertiveness and self-respect to change the rules and dynamics of their financial arrangements with men. Money, of course, often determines the power in a marriage; but even if the man is the one bringing home the bacon, that doesn't mean the woman shouldn't be an equal partner. The following chapters discuss both how to seek that equality, and how to respond if that doesn't happen.

CHAPTER FOUR

The Money Trap

I hear many horror stories from women trapped by money. Their pain is so acute that I wonder how they survive each day.

One woman, Nina, claims she wakes up every day ready to change her life, but goes to bed with the handcuffs just as tight. Nina probably will never leave her husband. She is fifty-three, and just can't break from the past.

"In one moment, it all seems so clear. I will tell him that I'm sick of being a prisoner, and that things must change. I will tell him that I want to have equal rights with our money, and that means seeing all of his statements, and being allowed to make decisions without always having to run them by him. I feel like such a child because of this, and I'm a grandmother. So I jump in the shower, and become convinced that this will be the day that I tell him. I become happier because I know that I

can remove this burden. But then I walk downstairs, and he's at the kitchen table, and I freeze. I make him his coffee, and I swallow my pride. Soon, he's off to work and I'm back to misery."

Some women, like Nina, will probably never unlock the handcuffs. But for every Nina there are dozens of success stories. Other women, like Glenda, break away entirely, and learn to survive on their own. Yet others, through extremely hard work, manage to reinvent themselves and their spouses, both. They build on whatever love and mutual appreciation that is there, and find a way to maintain an equal marriage. The cuffs are taken off, and both partners seem to live contentedly. When this happens, it's not because they're being saved by Prince Charming. It's because they have learned how to stand up for themselves.

Cindy is one of those success stories.

"I'm amazed at how much my life has changed. The day passes by, and I don't feel the horrible anxieties that used to haunt me in whatever I did. I never thought it was possible to break away from the handcuffs, but I learned that the more I stood up for myself, the easier it got. It's just the beginning period that's the roughest."

Women like Cindy have emerged triumphant because they dared to assert their rights. They learned how to communicate their needs, and learned what to do if those needs weren't met. But another important element of their emergence as full, independent women was their willingness to demand financial rights, as well. It was one thing to be able to confront and communicate with honesty; it was quite another to demand your share of the pie. Following is a list of those

78

rights, and why each one is relevant to removing the hand-cuffs.

Women have the right to share all financial decisions that affect their lives.

Here is the most crucial decision of all. From generation to generation, women have believed that the man has the right to make all the important financial decisions. If he made the money, he should determine how it is to be spent, right? Wrong. He made the money, but he is a partner in a relationship, and partners do things together. Nobody appointed him commander in chief.

Over the years, this is the right that women who come to see me fail to grasp more than any other. Naturally, that's because they've been conditioned since they were little girls to buy into the premise that the man *knows* more about money, and therefore he is in a better position to make responsible choices. Karen watched her dad handle the money in the family, and always assumed that was how it was done. Even when she became an adult, she saw no reason to change: She let her husband play the same role.

"I remember those times when we went out to get a new car. We'd go everywhere, maybe spending days and days looking for the right one. And then, finally, it was Dad who decided what we were going to get. Mom just sat there, and I knew that she wasn't crazy about the car. It was what he wanted, not what she wanted. But she said nothing. I just remember the look of disappointment on her face. Now I fear that my daughter sees the same look on my face."

But times have changed, and with women's increasing roles in the workplace, and the psychology of our times, they have begun to understand that money and power go hand in glove. To sabotage this change, men in the Golden Handcuffs will often devise very clever schemes to keep the women out of the money process. Sharon, forty, recalled what her husband, Mike, tried to do.

"One day, he came home and told me about an investment deal he had just agreed to put $8,000 of our money into. I was shocked, and told him that. We had worked hard for that money. Okay, technically he had worked hard for that money, but it was ours, and he had decided by himself to spend it on what I considered a rather tenuous deal. He apologized, but said that he hadn't had time to consult me, that he had a small window of opportunity in which to act. I looked at him, and I knew he was lying. That was the worst part of it."

Of course, Mike was lying. What kind of investment deal gives you such little time that you can't even consult your wife? Clearly, Mike was deeply threatened by her desire to share in financial decisions—and he is far from alone. What's important here is that women realize that this will be the toughest right to keep in their column; it strikes exactly at the core of what Golden Handcuffs are all about. If women can acknowledge this right and refuse to tolerate any relationship that doesn't contain it, they will go a long way toward ending their subservience.

I'm going to give a straight-from-the-gut opinion. I think that anyone who is involved in a relationship that encompasses the use of money is a fool not to understand the sources of the money, the use of it for expenditures, the method of gaining access to it, and the accountability system. Beyond understanding, I think it's equally important to have within the partnership equality of access of those funds. I'm talking about business relationships and interpersonal ones. You got married, and that was a contract under the law to abide by certain societal and perhaps religious rules. That is something you can accept, but it is equally important to understand that finances are a large part of that contract, also, even if clarification of that is not a part of the marriage certificate. Let's face it, finances can become a major aspect of a divorce decree. If you feel uneducated about financial matters, you can go to your husband and ask him to explain the details to you; however, it is highly likely, if you're reading this book, that this may not be the wisest course of action.

So, what are your options? Start at the bank, ask questions; go to the library, read; buy a book that you keep with you as a financial bible. In other words, take the initiative in educating yourself about finances.

When you feel that you have a grasp on financial lingo, then go to your husband and *tell* him you want to go over *all* the financial records. If he's too tired, or whatever the excuse may be, set a time within the next forty-eight hours to go over this information. If this sounds overwhelming, think of how overwhelmed you could be if he died or left tomorrow and you had to piece the puzzle together by yourself.

Sometimes it is necessary to go outside the marriage for help. Your husband won't necessarily be responsive, but you may not have all the answers. It is certainly no sin to see an expert. After all, it's your money, and you might as well do this job right.

But, strangely enough, a lot of women in the Golden Handcuffs are afraid to go to a financial consultant or economic advisor. Glenda explained:

"My husband would kill me if I did that. He would yell and scream that I didn't trust him, that I thought he would do something foolish with our money. And I kind of agree with him. What right do I have to do that? It is a sign of mistrust, and you might as well say there's nothing to the marriage if you do that."

I immediately set out to explain the facts of life to Glenda. I told her that she most assuredly *did* have the right, especially when all the evidence showed that Ken (her husband) either didn't know how to handle money, or else chose to squander it selfishly on his needs. Then I asked her how she would feel if he came home one evening, and said he had just seen a financial consultant, and felt their future would be a lot brighter now. Glenda's eyes lit up. "It would show that he cared enough about our future." I stopped her right away, and she understood: She had the same right as Ken did.

There are many ways to exercise this right. Banks are staffed with people who can provide that kind of advice, and the financial planning business has become huge in the last decade. Even if it might be somewhat expensive, usually the advice is well worth the investment. Equally important, it demonstrates a desire by both husband and wife to be partners in financial matters.

When I first encountered Jennifer she said, *"We've been married for five years, and I don't even know how many accounts we have at the bank. How do I know that he isn't hoarding money away in case we have trouble? How do I know what I'm entitled to? I ask him about it, and he says he just hasn't had time to acquaint me with everything. Hasn't had time? Is five years enough time?"*

One sabotaging technique is "Don't you trust me?" That's a really good one because it exploits the woman's natural tendency to want to make trust a big issue in the relationship. Women are furious when men don't trust them, so if a man accuses his wife of lacking trust, he's got a good chance of not having to deal with the real issue. Women want so much to trust the man. In fact, if they trust him, they'll settle for a lot of disappointments in their relationship. Men are clever enough to know this.

Naturally, a lot of women let the man stay in control. They are so uncomfortable with the prospect of changing their life that they'd rather remain ignorant, or they are afraid to confront the real issue of inequality of access to funds. Women are terrified that men are hiding the truth about their finances.

One such case was Janet. *"I know he's putting some away,"* Janet told me in one session. *"We used to have more money, and I know I haven't been spending it. I can, at least, keep track of that. Why don't I confront him? 'Cause I have no proof. And I know he'll just explode, and I don't want to face that. Maybe someday I* will *confront him."*

Janet may or may not confront him, though obviously she should: *Women should never accept these kinds of excuses.* They ought to make sure the man follows through on his promises to provide equal access to financial information. And there are several ways for the woman to do that— although in *all* cases she first must get the man to agree to a specific date and time for them to discuss their entire financial situation. If the man continues to stall about setting up that kind of discussion, the woman should demand to go with him to the bank, or to meet with their stockbroker. In other words, the woman must say that she is no longer willing to wait, that she will now physically enter his financial world.

This kind of threat terrifies the men in the Golden Handcuffs. At this point, many decide it's time to give in, that every sabotaging technique has failed. They'll finally agree to an appointment because nothing scares them as much as a woman escorting them into their special financial circle. It's trespassing. It's like interrupting an all-male poker game. For many men, controlling money is their last claim to the old notion of authority. Giving it up is all but impossible for some.

Some men will reveal bits and pieces—an account here, one there. But even more importantly, they generally will not willingly reveal everything. They will try to keep hidden the status of certain accounts or stocks, or provide misleading information. The point: He still feels he has control.

Why do men cling so desperately to this control? As we have discussed before, some feel that, without that grip, their women will see who they *really* are, and leave. Others, taking a cue from their fathers, have seen money as the way to compete against other men, and don't feel that finance is a woman's domain. In effect, the man doesn't want the woman to be on his team. What's so insane about this psychology is that in all my years of practice I have never seen a case in which the "team" wasn't strengthened by the addition of the woman.

But many men don't understand that. They'd rather do it on their own. Maintaining a monopoly on the money decisions in the marriage allows them to keep a safe distance from their spouses and continue to be territorial in at least one aspect of their relationship.

"He'd go off into a world of his own in our home office," Kate said about her husband, Ned. *"Hour after hour, he'd be working on the bills, and figuring out what we could afford. Whenever I came in, he quickly covered up his papers and gave me the message that he was busy. He complained about all the work, but I knew he was secretly happy. It was a chance to maintain some space from me, and I knew it."*

Women have the right to build financial security.

Hopefully, now that the women in the Golden Handcuffs have agreed that they possess the right to share and access relevant financial information, the next task is to start building financial security. Essentially, they have the right to save money for the future, for that rainy day when disaster springs out of nowhere. Even if they aren't the ones making the money, they are still the ones who would likely suffer most adversely from any hardships. In fact, studies have determined that when a marriage breaks up, it usually takes the man about three years to regain his past financial status. It takes a woman fifteen years. Big difference.

Yet, for all their preoccupation with money (it's how they compete in their world), men in the Golden Handcuffs often oppose the idea of keeping a substantial savings account. It is very threatening to them. They figure that if there's a lot of ready money in the coffers, then it's much more likely their wives will take half in any divorce settlement. John, forty, who was one of the men who came to see me on a regular basis, described that fear.

"I just felt she [Jenny] was going to clean me out. So I

decided I was going to do whatever I could to leave enough in there for emergencies, yet not so much so that she would have plenty to live on if we split. Whenever I'd get a little extra dough, I'd spend it on my toys—a boat, golf clubs, anything. I wanted her to need me. If she didn't need me, I felt, she would be gone."

The obvious question is: Wouldn't the woman feel less hesitant about leaving if she were going to be giving up an opportunity to keep living the good life? In other words, if there's no money there to keep supporting her, then why bother staying with a man who is so unsatisfying on all other fronts? The answer is that these women feel as if they have no choice. If they leave the relationship and don't have financial resources, they could wind up on the streets within weeks. If they don't have parents or relatives who will bail them out, then their man is their only support. So the insecure men manipulate the finances as a method of maintaining the Golden Handcuffs.

Interestingly enough, these same men do not want other men to know if they have meager savings. Acquiring money is a hotly contested game among men, and a small savings account is the sign of a loser. Instead, to show the appearance of wealth, they will spend money they really don't have. It's a false sense of power, but nonetheless one they crave. Other men will wonder how these fellows could have acquired a certain possession on a somewhat limited salary, and they'll respond, with all sincerity, "I just know how to invest." They just know how to *deceive*.

Through all of these defenses, however, a woman must demand that a savings account be established, and funded as regularly and fully as possible. At stake is her financial well-being—and if that isn't an obvious right, nothing is. If possible, a certain minimum should be agreed to by both parties, to be deposited every month, and the woman must ensure that this is done. If the man is unwilling to sacrifice enough to put aside for their future, the woman must come to the conclusion that he is not committed to *her* well-being. What about *her* future? *She's* the one who will likely be stuck in limbo if he loses his job or leaves her. He's got a skill; he'll somehow survive. What about her? Does she have a marketable skill? Hopefully so! If not, perhaps this is the time to evaluate how dependent she feels without one. Nancy finally asked herself some questions and came to her own conclusions.

"When Bob would play poker with the boys or spend money at the track, I kept thinking that there goes more money that we could use later on. Maybe I was a bit selfish; maybe I was thinking about money that I could use later on. I don't know. But the point was that he had complete disregard for that future; he only cared about his immediate gratification. Well, when I finally realized that this isn't a man who loves me, and that he was self-centered, I started making the moves to get out of there. It wasn't easy, but I left."

Women have the right to the fulfillment of financial need without guilt, begging, manipulation, or fear.

Often, women will get what they want regarding financial matters, but the price will be too high. They will get access to the financial decisions, or start to build a sound savings account, or share in every important move. But they will get those concessions in ways that cause psychological damage. They will lie, or cry, or manipulate. They will pull any trick in the book—and their book is pretty extensive—to get the man to give them what they want. Unfortunately, by winning the battle on these less-than-honest terms, they will lose the war.

The war is about their learning how to become assertive. In previous chapters, we've talked about how women must learn both how to criticize and how to say "no." Becoming assertive is what's needed to break free, and that same challenge must be faced when dealing with financial issues. One day, in the Golden Handcuffs group session, Helen argued with Kate about how Kate had finally gained access to the family's financial portfolio.

Helen: *"So how did you get him to show you the records?"*

Kate: *"Well, you know, I'd been trying for months, but finally, I just started sobbing like a baby the other night, and he must have felt badly. Because a few minutes later, he turned on the computer and forked over some information. I felt better, and knew I had won."*

Helen: *"You didn't win anything."*

Kate: *"What are you talking about? I know about all of our accounts now, and where I can get to them. How can you say that's not a total victory?"*

Helen: *"Easy. You cried. You begged. You lowered yourself. You weren't really willing to stand up for your rights as a woman. Plus, he didn't tell you everything."*

Kate did not respond. She just lowered her eyes in resignation. She always knew she hadn't asserted herself, but she had tried to hide it. She realized that unless she proclaimed her rights to her husband, nothing mattered and she certainly wouldn't unlock the handcuffs. A few weeks later, she went to her husband again. This time, she did not cry.

She told him straightforwardly that she wanted every little bit of financial information. He capitulated. This time it was a *real* victory for her, even though he grumbled and berated her for trying to "act like she knew everything." The important issue for Kate wasn't *his* emotional response, it was her honesty and straightforwardness with herself.

There are many ways in which women try to manipulate. One popular approach is to use the kids. Instead of asking the husband directly for her rights, she'll tell him that the children have been getting more nervous about the future and have asked those questions. Or she'll say she needs to know because she has become worried about their health. These may all be valid points, but they pale in comparison to the most valid point of all: The woman is a partner in the relationship, and has a *right* to know. Period.

Women will mention female friends and point out the financial rights *they* have. That misses the point, too: It doesn't matter what anyone else has; these are not rights by comparison—they are intrinsic to every woman, and should be respected enough to stand alone. "Women have the right to communicate their financial needs."

Logically, this right is the culmination of all of the other rights put together. Women must come to the realization that all of the previous rights make perfect sense—yet if they are unable to adequately communicate them to their husbands, the rights mean very little.

Here, the same rules of communication adopted in the issue of criticism can be applied. Essentially, the woman should firmly tell the man that she deserves those rights, and that if she doesn't get them, she and he may have to reevaluate their relationship. That may sound like a threat, but it is in fact a necessary warning to alert the man to the seriousness of these issues. Without giving respect to the woman's right to share equally in the financial end of the relationship, he is demeaning her, and he must understand that.

If a woman can't get these rights acknowledged (and not just pure lip service, but actual follow-through), then she must face the possibility that this is a one-sided relationship. She must of course first be certain that she did everything possible to strongly assert her rights, and that the man flatly failed to affirm them. She should also give him some time to make the adjustment, and should even try to put up with some of his sabotaging techniques. But if, over some weeks (or if necessary, months), he doesn't respond to the thrust of her grievances, then it's clear he isn't willing to surrender total control. And total control is what put those handcuffs on in the first place.

None of these rights will be easy to win. If they had been, they would have been granted a long time ago. Abandoning the handcuffs to a loving and trusting future is certainly a worthwhile goal. There are no guarantees here, and a lot of women go halfway and then back off; the truth is too threatening to them. They'd prefer to remain in the misery they at least understand, so they either accept defeat or allow the man to escape by just releasing a few insignificant details. "Hey," they figure, "that's better than nothing!" No, the *only* acceptable resolution is a full 50-50 partnership. Anything less is to allow one person to continue to control the other.

It is quite likely, of course, that by asserting these rights many of the women in the Golden Handcuffs will be ending their marriages. Only they can decide whether improving or rediscovering their self-esteem and dignity is worth that risk.

CHAPTER FIVE

Dreams, Goals, and Expectations

In order to have expectations, it is important to dream and set goals. To achieve them, your first major step will be to acknowledge that you have rights. For each woman, however, there may be a different pace, a different set of expectations and results. Therefore, it is important to set up a realistic time schedule for achieving the necessary goals to break the financial stranglehold. The women involved must map out, in progressive steps, which goals should be attained, in what order, and how long each of them should take. That way, progress can be more easily measured, and the women can gain small victories on their way to total liberation.

The problem, however, is that most of these women

have not set personal goals for decades, perhaps not since they were in high school or college. Then it was acceptable for them to do as well as possible academically. Males didn't seem to feel threatened by them. They didn't see the classroom as a natural battleground; this was one area where their egos weren't on the line. So the girls flourished, thereby demonstrating both intelligence and ambition. It looked like nothing would stop them.

Nothing did, except the need to be appreciated and loved—and in order to reach that objective, they set aside and/or forgot about their goals. For the women fated to wear the Golden Handcuffs, all the grandiose plans of attending graduate school and rising in the professional ranks gave way to the newest, most important reason for their existence: to please their man. *Everything* began to revolve around that goal, from polishing one's appearance to "giving in" on many matters to which they may have been opposed. Most of all, these women began to think constantly in terms of what *they* could do for *him*, not the other way around. Except with the issue of money. That became their reward—the sign that they were indeed being valued for their work. And so the cuffs were easily clamped on.

During the session in which the therapy group first came together, I went around the room and asked each woman for a list of her goals for the next six months, three years, and ten years.

Shannon: *"I'd like to see my husband move up in the company."*

Karen: *"I want to see my kids go to college."*

Marla: *"I hope my parents get along better."*

Marilyn: *"I want my husband's shirts to be pressed and out for him every morning."*

Helen: *"I want to have the house ready for him every night when he comes back from work."*

Gina: *"Everything should be in order for summer vacation."*

On and on it went. They spoke of their goals for everybody else *except* themselves. Not once did any of them definitively assert what they wanted for their *own* futures. One woman, in fact, began to talk incessantly about the guilt she was experiencing for failing to ask her husband's mother to move in with them. It was either that or a retirement home, and the daughter-in-law felt it was *her* responsibility to make that offer. Unbelievable—but that's what a lot of women do. They collect people they can take care of, because that allows them to avoid the realities of their own situation. If they look at their own pain and lack of fulfillment, they may also have to deal openly with their anxiety and depression.

The worst word in the English language for these women is *accountability*. If you're accountable for your pain and suffering, then you're also accountable for your growth and change. And who knows what demons will then arise from the dead! That's where setting goals comes in. It's the process by which women openly admit that they have assumed responsibility for changing their predicament. They have realized that their husbands may not change, and the only person they can control is themselves. The women must be their own agents of progress—and delay does nothing to improve their condition.

"Setting goals was my way of grading myself," said

Sharon, forty-seven, who after eighteen years of marriage finally unlocked the handcuffs. *"I was able to look at a piece of paper and see everything that I wanted to achieve, and it was a lot. But just having it there made me feel better. I wasn't going to complain any longer. I was going to act."*

The first thing I tell the women is to make a "wish list." That can encompass any desires they have in life, big or small. I tell them I don't want these wishes to be prematurely judged by what chance they have to be fulfilled. That is not my point here. Instead, I want them to see the *full* extent of their dreams, and how far their current course has taken them from even finding out if any of them is attainable.

Typically, however, as I mentioned earlier, these women have been trained for a long time not to think of *their* dreams. I remember one woman who *wouldn't* reveal her dream. When I persisted, she said "Oh, it's just frivolous. I'd love to be a jazz dancer." She only considered it frivolous because she knew that's what her husband would think.

It is important for these women not to incorporate their husbands' opinions into their dreams. Those dreams belong exclusively to them. They often believe that if they do dream, that means they can't be responsible for their husband or children. But the truth is that they can *do* their work at home, and still consider what might be important goals for themselves. Plus, acknowledging their dreams and fulfilling them can be the exact boost of self-confidence and self-esteem that they so desperately need. And if they feel good about themselves, then they will realize that they deserve the financial rights that will remove the Golden Handcuffs.

As mentioned in a previous chapter, these women use romance novels (or Geraldo, Oprah, etc.) as their escape from daily misery. Somehow, that's the only way they can allow contact with their deepest wishes and dreams.

Also, many times they see people whom they consider to be "really" suffering and it makes their life look better. Nancy, who read a romance novel a day, spoke for many women who found refuge in their dreams: *"My husband could mistreat me, or even abuse me. He could make me feel bad every day. But the one thing he could not do was take my fantasies away. Nobody could do that."*

With many of the women I've seen over the years, if they hadn't been able to escape via their dreams, I'm not sure that psychologically or emotionally they would have been able to survive. That's how they kept their sanity. But, over the years, their dreams have made them feel frail and helpless. When they were little girls they could fantasize about Cinderella, and it was all okay. It was even healthy. As adults, they are often ridiculed for idealistic dreams.

The objective of setting up goals, therefore, is to take the dreams from the land of fantasies into the world of realities. That doesn't mean that every last dream will come true. But at least they all will have a *chance* to be realized. Unless dreams are converted to real goals, they always remain just dreams.

Unfortunately for a lot of women in the Golden Hand-cuffs, that's exactly what happens. They remain so addicted to the *process* of dreaming that they aren't willing to relin-quish that and replace it with action. Each day, they can open the book or turn on the TV and escape once again rather than get down to the nitty-gritty of working out a plan of action. That feeling of renewal is what keeps them going, and they're afraid to give that up. But I remind them that they are forever destined to a double life of pain and escape until they make the mental transformation.

I ask these women five questions about their dreams, all designed to convert them to goals. Any woman wearing the Handcuffs should ask herself these questions:

How would you describe your perfect day?

The point here is to show these women the contrast between their ideal day and the painful reality of what the truth about it has been for so many years. Typically, many respond by laying out in wonderfully vivid details the kind of exciting day they'd prefer, but conclude by admitting (for example) "My husband would never want that kind of day." I usually state, "This is your dream. Your husband doesn't have to be there!" Once liberated from those shackles, the women reveal a *multitude* of dreams; it becomes difficult to stop them. It's as if a dam inside of them is finally breaking, releasing all the dreams that they felt could never come to fruition.

What do you want to achieve in your work life?

Many will respond initially by talking about the house-work—the chores. They get a blank look, as if I've spoken to them in another language. Nobody has asked them that question in years, maybe decades, and they certainly haven't asked it of themselves. But once they get the point and stick to their career aspirations, it's like they come alive again before my eyes. They'll talk about their former hopes to be a lawyer, or a graphic artist—whatever. The point is that they admit they want to do something besides serving.

Another clarification: Those women who are happy serving at home aren't usually coming in for therapy. Happy people don't usually seek therapists.

Dreams, Goals, and Expectations

How much money do you want from a job?

What's critical here is that these women realize that they *can* get paid for work. It seems like a simple concept to grasp, but for the women of the Golden Handcuffs, it's been years since they've been paid for work. Human beings feel a special sense of satisfaction in being compensated for the work they do. Men obviously have experienced that feeling for quite some time. Women have missed out, and many don't think they should continue to do so.

What kind of lifestyle do you want for you and your family?

The idea here is to bring their family back into the picture. I ask them where they want to live, and what kind of house they'd like. I tell them to close their eyes and not censor anything. Soon, these wonderful visions pour out, full of rich details about their innermost dreams. Yet, through all this imagery, something very strange often happens. Someone is missing from these dreams: their husbands.

This, of course, is no coincidence. The husband is not in the dream because the woman has realized that these goals are not possible as long as he continues to control her. That doesn't mean the husband can't regain a place in those dreams. But the woman starts to understand that it is *she* who must initiate the changes for the dreams to have a chance of coming to fruition. The husband may not feel the need to alter the status quo.

What would you do if you had more time?

To me, this question may be the most relevant because it strikes right at a woman's relationship to time. In her present routine, her time is not really her own; it belongs to her husband and children. As mentioned earlier in the section on learning how to be alone, when women in the Golden Hand-cuffs spend time on their own interests, they start to feel guilty. I'll never forget the day Kathy walked into my office with the biggest guilt trip I had seen in years.

"A few weeks ago, my husband was coming down to eat breakfast when I told him I was going to go with Suzie to her exercise class. My mother, who lives with us, thought I was crazy to leave without pouring my husband's cereal, but I left anyway. I was late, and I was excited about something for the first time in a long time. Later, when I got home, my mother was screaming at me. She said she never would have left her husband at the breakfast table, and certainly not without pouring his corn flakes. I was devastated. I felt controlled by my mother, my husband, and, most of all, by my own guilt. I just don't know how to get rid of guilt."

It took a whole session, but I showed Kathy that her mother was *not* right; that Kathy had a perfect right to sometimes place her interests above her husband's. Getting these women to put aside their guilt over such matters often is a most challenging task. They have to learn that internal validation can start to replace the often skewed judgment of others.

Finally, when they do accept the idea that they have a right to free time, the results are fascinating. Many just want to sit in a park and stare at the sky—and there's nothing wrong with that, at least for a while. But the thought becomes immediately threatening to them, and they look for ways to escape it. The most popular excuse is the family—"I've got to make dinner for the kids" and "I've got to take Johnny to soccer practice." The truth is that most of us have more free time than we think. Some women have gone to the extent of *adding* a list of familial responsibilities after our initial sessions, so they can point out reasons why they *can't* spend free time. Slowly, I teach them how to stop being responsibility magnets and allow time for themselves.

Once the dreams have been written down they become goals, and therefore potentially attainable. Now it's time to come up with a system for achieving them. Unfortunately, too often women follow the misguided approach of using a man's system to meet those goals. In other words, just because it may get great results in the workplace doesn't mean it will be the right method for the women of the Golden Handcuffs.

In the work environment, the system advocated by the "How to Succeed in Business" books is about becoming more productive for the employer, for *somebody else.* Sure, those who apply it may reap great financial rewards and bonuses, and maybe even promotions, but the underlying concept is that the employee has learned how to get more done for the welfare of *the company.* It really isn't about any kind of *internal* validation.

When women try that approach, they begin to see their husband as the employer. They are trying to achieve their goals and do a better job so that he will approve. That's because, to these women, the man *has* been the boss. He's the one who has had a monopoly on power in the relationship. He's the one who has punished them, and he's the one who has given them a bigger allowance when they've been good. But these women have to learn how to accomplish their goals without seeking anyone else's approval, without any judgments but their own. Otherwise, they will never really be free. Because even if the man does approve of the "new" wife, he still retains the power to change his mind at any moment, leaving the woman helpless all over again. Until we can feel comfort in our own validation, it will be difficult to be free.

"I still found myself trying to fit into his expectations," Gloria said after months of setting up her goals. *"Every time I felt like I had taken some steps forward, I felt pretty good, but then I looked over at him, and he didn't appear satisfied. So all the work I had done went out the window. This pattern kept repeating itself until I finally stopped myself and realized I had made changes. I was becoming more assertive. I was being more true to my dreams, and I wasn't going to let him stop them."*

The next step is to set up a realistic timetable to meet the new goals. These women are masters of procrastination. They'll come up with any reason to delay the implementation of any new approaches that might be threatening to them. They have a huge fear of success—even greater, in some cases, than the fear of failure. Their excuses are positively brilliant.

The best way for them to reach their goals is to go about it in incremental fashion. By breaking it down that way, these women are given a chance to feel graduated levels of success: Each time they succeed, it is easier for them to take the next step. Because of their insecurities, though, they are constantly looking for reasons to declare this experiment a resounding failure. Typically, when asked to achieve the most basic task, these women will often respond "I was so busy, I didn't have time to call" or "They never called back." Failure becomes a self-fulfilling prophecy: "See? I *knew* I couldn't do it," some women will say.

Dreams, Goals, and Expectations

Failure takes the burden of responsibility off of such women, who then go back to their life as it was, certain that they had tried their best, but that "It wasn't meant to be." They'll also use any roadblocks, especially early in the process, as signs that they did something wrong. For so many of these women, they've done this thing wrong their entire lives—and that's why they feel they _deserve_ to be unhappy.

In order to break that sort of psychology, I set up weekly goals. For the first week, I ask women to pick one of their dreams and do some initial research on it. For example, if a woman wants to take jazz dancing, I ask her to find out where the best class is held, and at what time and cost. When they come back and see me after a week, I expect them to have that information. Usually they do have it, and their sense of satisfaction is immediately apparent. They're amazed that they hadn't thought of doing it sooner.

I try to make sure that their legwork during the first week is done from the house, just using the telephone. This way, they don't have to deal with the trauma of leaving the house and stepping into an environment that they may perceive as threatening. Because they are so sensitive about failure, visiting a class too quickly might set them up for an easy rejection: "What if the teacher thinks I'm too old? Or too fat?" Just making contact on the phone allows the woman a greater sense of control and a lesser chance of failure. I call this stage _setting up a connection._

The next stage is _gathering._ Here, I tell them to obtain on-site information. For example, if the goal is to open a checking account, then this requires a visit to the bank to see what that entails. They haven't yet made an all-out committ-

101

ment, but they're getting closer. They will now know everything that's required to take the next step.

Finally, week three arrives, and it's time to *act*. Fortunately, most of the women, after achieving success during the first two weeks, find the third step to be easier than they ever imagined. They will sign up for that class they've wanted for years, or they'll open that savings account for something special. They are taking huge steps toward unlocking the handcuffs. "*I just drove into town and registered for jazz dancing*," said Chelsea. "*It was that easy. If I had only known sooner.*"

The fourth week is for rest. After all, these women have, in most cases, achieved quite a lot in just three weeks. They've done more in that time than in the previous three years. They are on their way! (I've heard others suggest that small gains should be made over the course of six months or a year, but I believe that is far too long to make things happen. If women wait that long, the chances of surrender or self-sabotage only go up.) The fourth week is also a good time to reflect on the next series of goals, the next three-week increments. Change is an ongoing process, and what these women are doing is setting up a whole new pattern of behavior: They are replacing servitude with assertiveness.

Will there be roadblocks? Of course, and they will crop up out of nowhere, constantly. Can the roadblocks stop the women from unlocking the handcuffs? Certainly, but only if they let them. Sometimes, to be sure, there will be roadblocks that can't be overcome *right away*, but part of the program is to understand that we can't *always* control every aspect of life. For instance, if the money isn't there for the jazz dancing class, the money *isn't there*. But that doesn't mean that the goal must be forgotten. All it means is that the woman puts it temporarily on the shelf and looks for a replacement. The next goal query obviously becomes: "How *do* I get the money for the class?" They are basically looking for the best way to view the problem. It's another sign of assertiveness.

Another advantage of slow, incremental change is that it won't shake up the household. Jennifer gradually turned her life around, and her husband never noticed a thing. Plus, because he didn't react adversely to her changes, that minimized the chances that he would try whatever sabotaging techniques he could find. Men *won't* sabotage if they don't envision any threat to their power, but in so many cases these women have been so fearful of their husband's reaction that fear has practically immobilized them from taking any action. Moving slowly cuts down on that fear.

"One week I checked out a class, and the next week I registered," Jennifer said. *"And then the next week, I was sitting in the classroom. I did it in such a way that he wasn't aware of the new woman I was becoming. That made things so much easier for me."*

One thing I *do not* endorse in trying to meet goals is a "demand list." Helen, fed up after so many years of mistreatment, finally went up to her husband one day, equipped with a long list of complaints. She was practically hysterical as she read off each of them. Her husband just sat there and waited for the tirade to end. Then, in just a few carefully selected phrases, he put out her fire, and she felt more defeated than ever. "It must be your time of the month," he said. "Don't I do enough for you? Don't I pay for everything you've got? You could be on the streets if it weren't for me!"

The message was clear: "If not for me, you would really

be in trouble, so you might as well put those demands away and get back in the kitchen." Which is exactly what a lot of these women do. What their husbands say makes them realize again how lucky they are that someone is taking care of them, even if this means that these women have to sacrifice so many of their rights. The approach of using demands also allows the man to react to the *way* the woman says things, rather than to what she actually says.

Men often placate. A man will listen to a woman's litany of disputes, and then carefully decide which of them he will resolve. Basically, he looks for the little victories he can give her, to shut her up. He realizes she's in one of those "moods" and she isn't going to stop ranting and raving until she at least gets *something* out of it. Ben, one of the men who came to see me on a regular basis, explained the psychology.

"I usually pick up about two or three things she's yelling about, and decide they are the ones I'll deal with. Of course, money is always a good remedy. I'll agree to give her $10 more a week for her allowance, and that usually shuts her up. It's pretty easy."

The men have won because now they can have some peace again. The women have won because they are desperately searching for *any* way to feel good about the marriage and themselves. They want so badly to be accepted that they'll take the victories, one small one at a time. Unfortunately, at that rate, they'll be a long time in the process.

Most of these problems continue because neither party has good self-esteem. As with so many other issues, having a solid belief in yourself is a huge factor when you are in the Golden Handcuffs. Ever since they failed to receive the proper amount of validation at home, these women have been caught up in the search for it. First, the boyfriends in high school were supposed to do the trick. Then the serious relationships. Then the husband, the Prince Charming who supposedly arrived to save the day. But *nobody* among them quite knew how to do it, and the women wound up back where they started.

Typically, these women believe that someone else will come along to enhance their self-esteem. No doubt the loving presence of another person makes us all feel good, and the subsequent loss of that person can be a huge blow to our feelings. But, for these women, external judgment is everything: "If my husband made more money, he'd treat me better." "If I had more money, I could get better clothes and I'd feel better about myself." "If I had a more prestigious job, I'd feel better." The point is that they need to search *within themselves* for the validation. Only then will they have the power they need to take off the handcuffs. As long as anyone else has the power to judge, he has *all* the power.

Throughout this book so far, I've explained the need for women to assert their rights and become fully accepted as equal financial and emotional partners in the relationship. I've also shown that at the root of their problems is their low self-esteem. But I'm sure a lot of women are caught in a contradiction: "I know I don't like myself, but how do I begin liking myself?" Following are some suggestions for that process.

Make a list each day of things you felt good about doing on that day.

It's amazing the responses I get on this one. In the group session, about 80 percent of the women will have trouble coming up with even one item to put on the list. They have programmed themselves to put a negative spin on everything that happens to them during the course of the day and they will ignore any development that could be construed in a positive manner.

I remember one woman saying to me that she didn't want to think positively because that would only get her hopes up, and she knew they'd be dashed sooner or later. These women are also afraid that if they start to look at things—and themselves—in a positive light, they'll then have to own the responsibility of making their lives even better. They won't be able to resign themselves anymore to the simple fact that they're not good enough for anything better, that they don't really deserve a fulfilled life. They won't be able to use that excuse further. So, instead, they prefer to keep seeing themselves as victims. Better that than the burden of actually trying to change the status quo.

But the list *is* important. It becomes written proof that each day, despite whatever its controversies and hardships, usually has something good in it. Soon, after this process is done day after day, the women realize that in fact many good things happen *all the time* to them. And if that's the case, then they can't really be the failures they thought they were. It puts a huge hole in their self-identity: *"After a while, I began to see that most of the things that happened to me were quite good,"* Keri said after months of compiling daily lists. *"It made me realize what a lie you can tell yourself if you really want to."*

Do at least one thing each day for your own personal pleasure.

This may seem like a simple task, but for the women of the Golden Handcuffs it can be an ordeal. Again, when I posed this question to the group, the results were staggering. About the same percentage (80 percent) couldn't immediately tell me even *one* thing they had done that day for their pleasure. Finally, when I persisted, they came up with *several* answers. Unfortunately, each of the tasks they brought up was something they had done with their husbands. (Translation: Things that were for their husband's pleasure, or that they did with his permission.) There was nothing they could recall that they chose to do on their own as free, independent women!

Women trapped by the handcuffs should start looking for things that will please them. Maybe it's a cup of coffee, or some ice cream, or a video they've always wanted to rent. It doesn't matter. What *does* matter is that they begin to see themselves as worthy of doing something *they* enjoy—regardless of anyone else's judgment.

Forgive yourself when you make a mistake.

Women who wear the handcuffs have trouble in this department. Regardless of how serious their "offense" was, they have taken it as if it's the end of the world. That's because they've been taught, ever since childhood, that they are *not supposed* to make mistakes. These women must learn that if they make a mistake, it doesn't mean they are horrible people. Yes, they are flawed—but so is everyone else. They've begun to believe that if they make too many errors they'll be completely rejected, and that paralyzes them constantly. So instead of standing up for their rights, they hold back, afraid of that one mistake that will *really* put them in emotional peril.

How can you learn to forgive yourself? The key is to take a more accurate look at the incident. What were your choices? Afterwards, write down all the things you like or dislike about yourself. Soon, you won't believe how many fine attributes you possess. Review that list constantly, especially when you make a mistake and think you're a worthless human being. Choose to correct the things you can and realize that making improvements is important. You simply won't be able to get rid of all the flaws, but that's okay. Accept them. Understand that they are a part of you, just like the things you like about yourself.

"I started my list one day, and I thought there would only be a few items," said Nellie. *"But I sat there for hours, and got excited every time I came up with something new. All these years, I thought I hated myself, but that wasn't true. That was just the story I chose to tell myself. But everything has changed now. I realize I'm pretty unique, and that has allowed me to seek the rights I deserve, and not accept an unequal relationship any more."*

Exercise and take care of your health.

I can't overstress the importance of exercise. Studies have shown that anyone who exercises takes a huge step toward dealing with emotional and psychological problems. After physical exercise, the brain begins to produce chemicals that act as antidepressants. Once the workout becomes a regular habit, you will realize that you have found a wonderful new way to do something positive each day. You'll feel good about not just your body, but also your entire being.

Even more important is the need to take care of your daily health needs. Many women I've worked with routinely ignore their health, day after day. When I asked them when the last time that they took their child to a pediatrician was, they can answer immediately. I ask them about their husbands, and they can quickly recite facts about his health regimen as well. But when the question is posed, "When is the last time *you* went to the doctor?" they give a sheepish smile and say they've been meaning to make a doctor's appointment but they just haven't had time.

Of course, neglecting their bodies is another example of the degree to which women can devalue themselves. They put everybody else first, but they have to understand that they can treat themselves well *without* sacrificing everyone else's welfare; that there is no reason to feel guilty about monitoring one's own health. Unless they show a higher regard for their own health, how can they expect anyone else—especially their husbands—to respect them?

I'm not talking only about going on a diet. In fact, diets can be counterproductive. The need to lose weight can become a horrible obsession which will do nothing to unlock the handcuffs, but rather will transfer all the pain of the woman's life to her quest to lose weight. And it's a diversion that might not have an escape hatch. What I'm talking about is the idea of eating properly by taking in the right amount and kinds of food. All these women have to do is visit a nutritionist who will recommend what to eat. The results *can* be quick, and *will* carry over to all other areas of their lives.

Natalie had neglected her health for almost twenty years. One day she went to see a nutritionist and later started exercise and weight training. Then everything began to change.

"Almost right away, I felt I could do anything. I started to feel stronger all over my body. I wasn't helpless anymore. I wasn't some patsy that could never offer any resistance. The food I ate became an extension of the new person I was

*becoming. I didn't feel weak around him. I felt I was his match,
and maybe more."*

In most cases, the husband won't even notice the wife
who exercises and sees a doctor more frequently. Again, any
positive changes that can occur without worry over the man's
reaction is highly preferable, at least until the woman has
developed the courage to confront him on the issues that
have made her so unhappy. Plus, exercising can be done with
a partner, which gives those who have become introverted an
opportunity to begin establishing friendships.

Find a model.

Find someone whom you would like to emulate. A great
place to look is the local public library. Just go up to the
information desk and ask for a book about a strong-willed
woman who overcame great odds to assert her independence.
There are countless biographies that fit that description.
Many women complain that they don't know *anyone* who has
done what they're trying to do. That may be true. Yes, most
of their friends usually *are* in a similar predicament; they have
the handcuffs, too. But that is why these women must go
beyond their immediate circle to locate that model.

It isn't necessary to become that model woman. All you
have to do is study her life, and find out how you can adapt
her strengths to your own situation. Read the book for inspiration: "Yes, I *can* change my life." And don't worry about
your husband. Here, again, he won't care which books you
are reading. "What are you doing, honey?" "Oh, I'm reading
the life story of Amelia Earhart." "Oh, that's interesting."
And he'll go back to reading the sports page. He'll forget he
ever asked.

In most cases, avoid making the model a member of

your family. Instead of taking a chance by using such a familiar (but potentially problematical) person for inspiration, the woman in the Golden Handcuffs should make an outside model her symbol of validation. What she is doing, in essence, is taking the power for validating her self-image that she used to surrender to her husband, and giving it to herself by using a model. Ultimately, that is the main purpose of having a model: learning to give *yourself* the power. That's how these model women overcame great odds by themselves: They didn't give the responsibility to someone else.

It is better when the model doesn't know she is *your* model. You don't want a dialogue between the two of you, because then you run the risk of perceiving rejection by her and crushing whatever progress you might have made— perhaps preventing you from ever trying again. Thus, you must choose with care. (That's not to say, however, that family members *never* are useful for this purpose. But it's still far better to pick someone you will never actually meet.)

Take chances.

Most of the steps we've talked about have involved some element of risk. That is natural: You are asking yourself to stop a whole pattern of behavior, built up over so many years, and try something different. This can be frightening. "How will my husband react? How will my children react? How will I react? These mysteries have stopped many women from making the necessary changes—but they were probably not ready, anyway. The important thing to understand is that one would have to be very odd, indeed, for these thoughts not to arise.

And there is no way of getting around the truth—the new behavior *is* very risky. You might lose your husband.

You might lose a whole circle of friends. And, perhaps most frightening of all, you might lose the person you thought you were. But remember this—you were miserable in the marriage. You felt less than whole. You had abandoned the person you used to dream of becoming when you were a young girl.

Whatever positive changes you do make will improve your life in the long term. You will no longer feel you are making all the compromises for everyone else. You will no longer feel that you don't deserve time for yourself. If your husband can't adapt to the new you, that is *his* problem. That might make your life difficult in the short term, especially financially. But, in the end, it will all be worth it.

The women in the Golden Handcuffs must remember that the only way to build self-confidence is to take chances. They can't run from that challenge. They must *embrace* it.

"It was terrifying at first," recalled Sandra. *"I kept waiting for disaster with every change I made. Who was this person? So many times, I thought, 'Forget it, I'm going back to the old me.' But the truth is I* was *going back to the old me. I was going back to the person I was before I got married, before I thought I needed to be rescued. I didn't* need *to be rescued. That was just a story I told myself. I don't tell that story anymore."*

CHAPTER SIX

Assert Yourself

Okay, now you feel better about yourself. You're taking a class. You're spending time alone. You're valuing your health. You're beginning to do all the things that a caring human being should do for herself. And all these changes have allowed you to reassess the relationship—especially the financial arrangements that you have made.

We've already discussed the need to gain access to the money, and to share the information. But there are a host of financial rules that must be addressed. I bring them up only now because it is important for women to establish a higher self-esteem first—before they can truly understand them. Coming from a great source of inner strength will allow women to be assertive, and not constantly surrendering to another's wishes. These rules are important even if you're *not* married, because money, as we have so often learned, comes into play in almost all walks of life.

Always keep your checking and savings account solely in your name when you are not *married.*

This is purely about power, which women must be careful not to surrender. I have seen too many women relinquish total control of their accounts before marriage. Would you surrender money in a business deal without a contract? Once you do that, you begin to lose the power of making decisions. If, later on, he becomes abusive or you're just unfulfilled in the relationship, the fact that his name is on your accounts may restrict your ability to get out of the relationship or may leave you responsible for his debts. Even if you are having a wonderful time because you are living together and not married, and you feel you are deeply in love, your accounts should remain in your name only. Later, if marriage results, then the required financial moves can be made.

Most men who are not married really enjoy this game of playing house. Essentially, the man often does not equate it with meaning that the couple is ready to get married. The woman, however, usually sees it as the next closest thing to marriage—and, hoping to show her faith in the man, may be willing to surrender more control than is advisable. The man may also exploit the trust issue: "Don't you trust me? If *I* had the money in reserve, I'd share it with *you*." Helen trusted her lover, and lived to regret it.

"I had $40,000, and I kept saying no when he said we should share it. Finally, one day, I relented. We were so in love, I just figured nothing could go wrong. In nine months, everything went wrong. He started sleeping with another

woman, and soon, we were history. So was most of my bank account."

Never give him the money you brought into the relationship for him to invest, just *because he claims to know more about money than you do.*

Women must remember that as soon as money is handed over to him it becomes community property. Too often, you can lose all control of your money. At best, you are at the mercy of your husband and his lawyer in the event of a split.

Never allow one of his relatives or friends to take control of your money.

Often the man is very certain that the woman stays with him only because she needs him financially. Many times a man feels threatened if the woman knows more about money than he does, but sees nothing wrong if the reverse is true. So, if he recognizes that he's not the most brilliant money manager, he'll enlist help from his own family to protect his power base.

Using someone from the family basically allows the man to preserve control. It's the ultimate slap against his wife that he'll go to a relative before he will turn to her. This way, he can benefit from the family's help, yet keep her from showing him up. It's an ego thing, too; these men simply believe that it is their role to handle the money. She can pay the bills, but he really makes the decisions. Women should insist that extended family members are kept out of their finances.

Do not agree to an allowance.

This may be the most important rule. As we've discussed earlier, accepting an allowance gives the man an incredible amount of control over the woman, establishing the same kind of dependent relationship she had with her father. Recently, I pointed out this problem to Katherine, and she vowed she'd make an immediate change. Two weeks later, she bolted into my office, proclaiming victory.

"I was so happy I was able to deal with this issue. I calmly made my points and told him I wasn't going to tolerate the situation any longer. He listened intently and told me he was giving me $75 a week. So now I get $75 a week instead of $50."

I couldn't believe what she was telling me. It's not the *amount* of money that matters, I told her. It's the fact that you are on his payroll, and therefore not an equal in decision making. The allowance keeps such women from tackling the essential problem; it is an easy way out for both parties. Furthermore, this is exactly what causes women to hoard money. Jennifer was a prime example of this practice. For years, Jerry gave her $50 a week, and she was amazingly adept at knowing how to stretch that out for herself and the kids. Plus, she was able to put away a few dollars every week to build up a secret pile for herself. This has been a centuries-old method for women.

"I've got almost $2,000 in my cookie jar," Jennifer said one day. *"It's almost all in $5 and $10 dollar bills. I normally don't use it unless there's a big emergency. I just like to know it's there."*

It may be there, but it doesn't solve the problem. First, the women still aren't asserting their rights. Second, the women still feel a tremendous amount of anxiety because of that imbalance. Third, the man is still in control, and feels an underlying lack of respect for the woman because of the way he's been able to dominate the relationship financially. And finally, it just gives the man another excuse for exercising his power: "What do you mean that you need money for sandals? You should have saved up for that." That is exactly something her father said to her 20 years earlier. The woman is still the little girl. This may be a matter of semantics, but if both parties determine a budget for *both* to follow, then the issue of equal power is resolved.

Always keep enough money in the bank so that you could survive for at least three months without him.

Too many women fail to prepare for this contingency. Instead of leaving an unbearable situation, they therefore have no choice but to stay on and continue to suffer day after day of mistreatment. Women in these kinds of relationships have got to keep in mind that any number of disasters could happen at any moment. The man could die, or run off with a younger woman; or she might be in so much pain that she can no longer sleep in the same bed with him. Whatever the case may be, the women in the Golden Handcuffs should put aside enough money for a minimum of three months. Clara did not, and suffered the ultimate disgrace.

"Things got so bad that I somehow got up the courage to walk out. I stayed with a friend for a few days until I could get my bearings and figure out the next step. The only problem was that I didn't have the money to get an apartment, and I quickly figured out that I wasn't going to get a job immediately. Soon, what little money I did have started to run out, and there was nowhere to turn. I moved back in with my husband. When I got to the door, he had this smug smile on his face, as if he had known all along that I wouldn't be able to make it without him. And I kind of agreed with him."

Three months is not a long time, but it's long enough for

prepared women to plot their next move. A sufficient financial cushion allows them the freedom to make choices. Instead of falling back into their old patterns of dependency, they can start a new life, knowing that they will have a place to sleep and food to eat. That might be just the difference between a future of possibilities and the familiar, unsatisfying status quo.

In fact, all women, regardless of *how* secure their marriages seem to be, should consider the realities of possible sudden changes in their situations. It's usually not easy to find work quickly, and it takes a lot of money to survive on your own and still avoid the streets. So they should constantly be aware of how much they've got, in case there is any sudden crisis in the relationship. This could be anything from unemployment to a sudden death. (How much will I need for rent? How much for food? How much for medical coverage? The figures should always be in her mind.) Three months is about how long it will probably take her to find work, and then figure out her *next* budget.

Following all of the financial rules and learning how to exercise these new and exciting rights might *still* not be enough to fix your marriage. Obviously the man might resist, or at least prove incapable of adapting sufficiently to your new emotions and powers. You might try everything, yet he might yield very little. The option of leaving a marriage is a very difficult step and one that, I believe, should be explored after you have encountered failure at attempted changes.

Often, before these people totally give up, they see one final resort, one place where maybe they can save the marriage—therapy.

As I explained in the beginning of the book, this is not an easy admission for these women to make. As much as they want to heal the emotional scars, they are terrified of receiving the cure. Because the cure means that they can no longer live in ignorance and denial and that they will never be able to look back.

But how do you know when it's time for therapy? How do you know when you've exhausted all other possibilities and it's time to bring in a complete stranger to fix your life? The answer is neither obvious nor automatic, since each individual situation is different. The reality is that the time for therapy was years ago before the problems multiplied, but that is not the way most couples function. Yet, among all the troubled women in the Golden Handcuffs, there is an unmistakable commonality, a shared horror at how such wonderful dreams have turned into such disturbing nightmares. They get up morning after morning, and the truth still has not gone away. They do not feel happy with their lives and they have lost hope of its changing. When they know the situation is not going to get better, it's time for therapy. Lisa knew.

"The worst incident happened last summer when he had me buy a revealing two-piece bathing suit. I was embarrassed to wear it outside our backyard, but if it pleased him, then I liked wearing it. When the office swim party was announced, I told him that I needed to get another bathing suit. He told me the two-piece would be 'great' for the party. I told him no. I didn't want people staring at me. The suit was just for him.

"He kept insisting, and finally I gave in and said I would wear it. This seemed to make him happy, and he kept talking about how all the other wives at the party would be jealous of my figure. I knew I should have remained firm and said no, but

he would've gotten angry and not talked to me for days. He accused me of not wanting to be with him at the party. I tried to explain that the reason was that I didn't want to wear that bathing suit at the party. I would be embarrassed. Finally, I gave in and let him have his way, rather than getting into a big fight. But even after I gave in, there was the nagging suspicion that his reasons for wanting me to wear that particular suit were more than he was telling me.

"At the party, everyone was out by the swimming pool and Richard [her husband] couldn't wait to have me get my cover-up off. I couldn't wait to get into the water. I started talking to Jennifer, the wife of one of the men in Richard's department. She seemed embarrassed at first, but after several glasses of wine, Jennifer told me that for the past week, Richard had been bragging in the office about what I would look like in the bathing suit. The information came from her husband.

"My worst fears were being realized. My wearing the bathing suit was so that he could be a center of attention. At that moment, noises from across the pool caught my attention. There was Richard, with a group of men from the office, pointing at me! They were all staring at me! Richard was acting like a strutting rooster. Just when I thought it couldn't get any worse, Linda, another wife, swam over, shook her head, and gave me a dirty look. I felt the tears beginning. I was never so humiliated. I knew at that point that I was no more than a possession."

Two days later, Lisa was in my office for the first time.

Often it requires a humiliating kind of event to force a woman to take steps she should have taken years ago. For Lisa, the bathing-suit incident was not really an unusual occurrence; her husband had been treating her as a toy since they were married fifteen years earlier. But, finally, the total humiliation of one experience will be the catalyst necessary to push someone over the top. Five minutes after our session had begun, she was in tears, telling the details of the bathing-suit story and many others that had occurred over the years.

Actually, though, for Lisa and so many other women in the Golden Handcuffs, events like these are a blessing. Otherwise, if the mistreatment and lack of respect from their husbands had continued to take place in smaller, unspectacular doses, these women might have remained passive forever. Internally, they might have felt the pain and hurt, but no single event would have justified a final emotional explosion. The bathing-suit incident made Lisa realize that her husband was *not* going to change. Or, perhaps, even more accurately, it made her realize that *she* desperately needed to change.

"I've tried to deny the truth for so long," she told me on that first visit. *"I kept thinking that maybe things would be different, that I was trapped in one long terrible dream that was bound to end sometime. And every time that he did something nice, I felt the handcuffs were going to disappear. I was wrong, and that whole scene at the swimming pool convinced me that if I didn't get some professional help, nothing would ever change. I felt so demeaned."*

A word of caution: As in every other profession, there are some therapists who are very competent, and some who are not. Because of their undeniable vulnerabilities and their willingness to surrender power to *any* male authority around them, the women of the Golden Handcuffs are especially susceptible to a seemingly calm and supportive type of man. That's who they thought their husband was, and now that's who they hope their therapist is. Too many women completely surrender to the male therapist, granting him far too much power. The women must remember that *they* are the ones who must do the work and live with the consequences.

When picking a therapist, these women typically go to their physician or gynecologist and seek a referral. That's a good start, but not enough. Women in the Golden Handcuffs should compile as much information as possible about the therapist. What is his/her degree? Where did he/she go to school? Find out if your doctor has referred other patients to the therapist, and what the results were. Were there any complaints? Would your doctor send a member of his/her own family to this person for therapy? If possible, try to speak to one or more women who have seen the therapist.

Although these women need to be assertive in this selection process, obviously their lack of assertiveness (with the husbands) is why they need a therapist in the first place. To compensate, the women should just go with their instincts: "Does this person seem like someone who can help me, someone I can trust?" If the answer is "yes," or even "maybe," it is time to proceed. Remember, these women haven't lost their intuitive powers—they've just put them on the shelf.

Once the therapist has been picked out, I highly recommend that the women in the Golden Handcuffs opt to join a group, perhaps in addition to individual treatment. That's not to say that one-on-one consultations won't be helpful, or even preferable, at certain times, but there are advantages to the dynamics of group therapy, and that should be part of the process.

Janice had suffered her agony alone for many years

before she finally summoned the nerve to see a therapist. Her first day in a group was a wake-up call.

"I had assumed that I was the only one with the handcuffs on. Even when I had talked to my girlfriends, they didn't sound like they had the same problems. But, after seeing other women around my age say the exact words that I could have spoken, and having the same look of resignation in their eyes, I knew I was certainly not alone—and I can't tell you how relieved I was. I wasn't crazy, after all. It wasn't my fault. I knew it would take a long time to deal with all the problems, but knowing I would have the other women praying for me made a huge difference."

Group therapy is usually far less expensive, so if money is a determining factor, which it usually is in these cases, then group work may be the best choice.

It is also important to find out the therapist's basic philosophy. What these women do *not* need is the Freudian approach, by somebody who wants them to slowly dissect everything that has happened in their lives since childhood. The past, of course, *is* relevant, but it is not the only area of analysis. We want to get into the past, but then get *out* of it. We don't want to make camp there. Remember, events from the past can never be changed, and the sooner everyone realizes it, the better. Spending long sessions pondering what Gloria said to her father in 1968 isn't going to solve anything.

These women should be looking for someone who is *behavior-oriented*, who will deal in the *present*. Of course, the past will be mentioned, but this therapist will concentrate on the progress the woman is making—on what kinds of steps she can take to change her life. And nobody involved should predict instant success. It will take months—maybe years—before real change takes place. To be dealt with here are emotions that the women haven't faced in many years, and these simply won't spill out in perfect order, overnight or in any specific time span. Each person responds differently. If after even just a few visits it doesn't seem that any progress at all is being made, don't hesitate to switch therapists. There is no time to waste here.

I advise women not to tell their husbands that they are seeking therapy if they think he will feel threatened or sabotage their efforts. Many times he will refuse to subsidize the trips, or, if he does allow them, will take active steps to otherwise undermine the woman. Before, when the woman was trying to rally support for her cause through a neighbor, that was irritating to the husband, but hardly a threat. But getting help from a trained professional frightens him. He is afraid that the therapist will validate his wife, and that thus the dynamics of the marriage will change forever. Many men will say or do *anything* to preserve their power. I recall one husband calling me up (in a state of panic) trying to destroy his wife's credibility: *"Dr. Olshan, my wife is crazy. She is certifiably nuts. She roams around the house like a wild woman, and I just think you should know that."*

The woman was certainly not crazy; the husband was trying to do anything to stop her progress. After he made up his story, he then asked how she was doing. He wanted to hear the specifics. Of course, I told him that I couldn't reveal that kind of information, and he was very frustrated. On another occasion, a different husband complained, *"My wife is getting nothing from her sessions with you, but doesn't want to hurt your feelings."* Fine, I thought—but that's something *she* must tell me; and if it's true, she should stop coming.

Men also think they can interfere by meeting with the therapist. "Okay," they reason, "I'll come in and straighten this guy out." Sometimes they'll even link up with other men in a group session, hoping to get rid of this therapy junk once and for all. But invariably the discussion shifts to how the *men* feel, and the issue of the women becomes secondary. Male groups are very effective, and I try to encourage as many women as possible to get their husbands involved. Not right away, of course (the women need enough time to begin changes), but after a certain amount of progress has been reached, it may be just the perfect time to get the men involved.

"For the longest time my husband resisted," Sharon said. *"He didn't take seriously what I was doing, but when he realized that I was determined to make changes, he decided to check it out for himself. And, in the beginning, he told me he didn't say much. But, as time went on, he realized that his insecurities had been partially responsible for the handcuffs that I felt. He worked hard on his insecurities in therapy, and our marriage became a lot stronger. He also said he didn't feel as stressed because we were sharing responsibilities, but he never knew that could happen."*

Before choosing a therapist to help unlock the handcuffs, a woman should also make certain that this person will be available. These women are likely to face all kinds of anxieties as they try to change the patterns that put them in their personal prisons. To alleviate tension, they may sometimes need to call when there is a crisis. They don't want a machine or a substitute; they want the person they have trusted.

So—now that the therapist has been chosen, it's time to set up the guidelines for the group. The group, at least in the first few months, is the most important sanctuary for the woman in the Golden Handcuffs. She obviously has decided that she can't talk to her husband. Her family isn't likely to provide answers, and her friends can't be helpful, either—as sympathetic as they might be, they're usually either not in her situation or if they are, they also have not found a solution. The women in the group are, however. They are facing the same demons and need the same reinforcement.

But even the group isn't always a sanctuary. I know of therapy groups wherein the women banded together to verbally attack the weakest link, the one victim who couldn't cut it in front of everyone. Often, they take out their frustrations on her, and the scene can get pretty ugly. If this begins to happen, the message to her is obvious: Get out now! Find a group that *is* supportive, that will allow momentary vulnerabilities, one that will stick with you for the duration. You have the right to be respected in the group. Different women will make changes at different paces, and the whole group has to recognize that. Also, make sure the group isn't too large. When there are more than about eight to ten women, very little can be accomplished. There isn't enough time that can be set aside for each woman.

Typically, the women in the group are getting honest feedback from other women for the first time in their lives. In adolescence, their girlfriends didn't know what to tell them. In adulthood, their friends were afraid to tell them the whole truth; it would have been too painful. And they certainly weren't going to discover much about themselves from their husbands. These women should seize the opportunity to learn as much as they can from the other women in the group. They need as many allies as they can find.

It is important that those trapped by the handcuffs acquire an *intellectual* understanding of their predicament. For years, of course, they've known *emotionally* what was happening, but by gaining a more objective insight they can determine why certain events have taken place, and understand the dynamics of their relationship. Group therapy is perfect for this purpose. The women, as long as they aren't abusive, can help analyze each other's lives—why certain behavior worked, and why other kinds backfired. They can do so without serious risks to the woman under scrutiny.

"At first, I resented all the interference," Kathy recalled. *"I mean, what right did they have to tell me how to run my life? But it was precisely because they didn't know me before that they could be free enough to tell the truth. And, soon I couldn't get enough of their input. I don't know where I'd be today if it weren't for them."*

Therapy is only an aid—it is not the whole cure. It is up to them to pick up the rest of the slack. Many women don't realize that. They seem fine for the hour or two in the group, but they are helpless the rest of the time. Therapy will mean nothing without follow-up, without a firm awareness that they must do most of the work. It's likely their husbands won't change immediately, the past won't change, and the dynamics won't change. *They* must be the instrument of change.

Whether they seek therapy or not, the women find other ways to empower themselves. We've already discussed the way they stash money, convincing themselves that this secret proves that they have power in the relationship. They have thus been crafty and manipulative—not totally weak. However, theirs has been a false sense of power, an indication that they have lacked the courage to assert *real* power. Money is not the only vehicle they can find for playing that game. Another is sex.

Helen realized this early on in her marriage, and after feeling degraded for years, she decided to fight back in the only way she could.

"He knows when I'm mad because he doesn't get any. I'll tell him I have a headache or I'm tired, but he knows that it's a lie. He knows that I am holding back because of something he said or did. And, after cutting him off for a few days, he comes crawling back. His tongue is hanging out and he looks like a little boy who lost his favorite toy. He then lets me have anything I want, and boy, do I stick it to him. I show him a lesson that he doesn't soon forget."

What lesson? Helen actually believed that she was assuming control in the relationship through her manipulations with sex. But nothing could be further from the truth. That's because while the immediate impact of Helen's behavior was her husband handing over a few goodies (usually a new dress or a larger allowance), the long-term fallout was that the two of them had developed a relationship based on passive-aggressive behavior. Her husband continued to treat her like a trophy. He still controlled all the bank accounts, and told her what friends she could have, and how she should spend most of her day. He was still taking over a parental role, and that didn't change no matter how many times she used sex as a weapon.

Using sex as a weapon demeans the woman and does

nothing to enhance the relationship. It is telling her that the only way she can get anything she wants is by withholding sex. This way, the woman is never going to undertake the more substantive—and challenging—internal changes that can finally fulfill her. Using sex won't do it. It only buys time, and makes her life a little easier. It doesn't *change* her life. It doesn't allow her to become the full-fledged, assertive woman who is hiding underneath all that manipulation.

Some women will go even further. They will have an affair, believing that this is the ultimate revenge. Carol met John one afternoon at the supermarket. He was a clerk there, and she was desperate for attention. They started an affair.

"I feel so good about myself now. I have finally found someone who treats me well. He's the man I thought my husband was. He buys me stuff without any conditions, without me having to make compromises. I want to be with him from now on."

When I hear that kind of response, I ask the woman having the affair to make a list of reasons why the lover makes her feel good when the husband doesn't. I want her to clearly understand how the husband has failed to address her needs. I also want her to recognize the affair for what it is: an escape from the reality at home, not a permanent answer to her lack of fulfillment. Some women, unfortunately, are merely exchanging one problem for another. They just don't know it yet. And, by surrendering power to yet another man, they are again avoiding the changes they have to make.

The choices are clear for these women. They have the ability to take off the handcuffs. Having an affair will not solve their problems. Therapy gives them a chance.

CHAPTER SEVEN

Make Changes and Move On

One thing is for sure: No matter how much the woman tries to fix her situation (and herself), and no matter how much the man may make an effort to accommodate her, there is no guarantee that the results will be positive. If the woman is changing herself, then who she becomes may not be someone who is attracted to, or even fond of, her mate. The person who thought she was in love with him is dead, replaced by a more assertive model, and there is no going back. The man may make most of the changes, and she will realize that he now is not the person she wants. Many times, however, they both make changes that allow them to feel better about their relationship and themselves.

I have treated countless women in the Golden Hand-cuffs who made some incredible progress over a number of months. They learned how to say no. They learned how to spend time on their own without feeling guilty. And they learned how to confront their husbands and gain total access to all pertinent financial records. They took just about every step possible to become assertive women.

Yet some of these same women were unable to take that *final* step. Either they were still afraid of the financial conse-quences or they worried about the emotional toll on them and/or their children, in the face of a formal separation. Whatever the case, instead of facing the truth, they resigned themselves to even more disappointment.

Unfortunately, there are few places for them to get help at this point, except if they've been physically abused. There are shelters, of course, that deal with battered women, that give them a temporary place of refuge while helping them put their lives back together. But what about those who suffer from the deep *emotional* scars? Just because the woman doesn't have a black eye doesn't mean she's not in incredible pain. She can be hurting just as profoundly as the woman with bruises all over her body.

When I know a woman is on the verge of leaving her husband but can't quite gather the nerve to escape, I make sure I put her in touch with others who have survived that ordeal. They explain to her that the reality isn't quite as terrifying as a woman is inclined to think. The troubled women greatly respect this advice.

"I was really scared until Annie calmed me down," said Belinda. *"She told me about all of her fears before she finally left her husband, and they are the exact ones I had. She told me*

how she had hesitated for almost two years, and those are two years she can't get back. After talking to her, I realized I had no time to waste. I had tried everything. It was time to leave."

I recommend that before they leave home, the women ask themselves some questions to determine whether they have exhausted all of their moves and resources, and yet are still denied the equality they have demanded. Often, if the women haven't gone over this kind of checklist, they invariably either exchange one set of handcuffs for another, or return to the same man. Because, despite all the progress they've made, they are still susceptible to their fears and vulnerabilities. They will ask themselves over and over: "Is it my fault? Is it I who can't change? Is it I who has ruined this relationship?" Looking at an objective checklist can show these women whether they have indeed done all that they could. The following are some of the questions these women should be asking themselves.

Have I confronted my husband?

This doesn't mean whether you have repeated your litany of woes, to make sure he's gotten the message. If you've seriously considered leaving the relationship, it's a pretty good bet you've had some serious arguments. No, this asks whether you have given an ultimatum: "Either you straighten up, or I'm out of here!" Most men, unfortunately, either ignore a woman's complaints, or placate her in order to shut her up. Few listen completely to her points. Unless, of course, there's an ultimatum attached to it all. And he has *got* to understand what's at stake here.

"I knew I finally had his attention when I told him I would leave him if he didn't work on making changes in our relationship," Gloria said. *"I knew it because, for the first*

time, he turned off the Raiders game and looked at me. It wasn't that distant look that had grown so familiar, where he was paying 50 percent attention to me and 50 percent to the football game. I had his total attention. He knew I was dead serious."

Think about this. Do your children always listen to you when there's no reward or punishment? If you threaten them and never carry out your threats, do they walk all over you? Consider that even when it is an adult who thinks he has all of the power, he probably won't listen unless you give him some reason to do so.

Have I put a time limit to my ultimatum?

An ultimatum without a time factor can be pretty weak. The women in the Golden Handcuffs have got to make their demands, and then give their husbands a reasonable amount of time to change. "Reasonable," of course, is open to question; it depends on each woman. I would recommend no fewer than three months, no longer than six. That gives the man enough time to learn how (and it *is* a learning process) to respect his wife and treat her as an equal partner.

Failure to give a time limit, however, feeds right into the woman's insecurities and tendency to procrastinate. This is a tough decision, maybe the toughest of her life, and, naturally, she wants to put it off as long as possible. The husband may exploit this weakness. He'll come to her with his sad eyes and slumped expression and basically beg for leniency. Many women buy this act and give the husband extension after extension—and soon their ultimatums bare no fangs at all.

The time limit must signify an actual physical separation. In other words, if she says she'll give him three months to change, and he doesn't, the final day is the last one by which he or she should be moving out of the house. And this physical separation is critical: It makes the necessary statement that she has tried everything and it just hasn't worked. The *only* exception to following through on the ultimatum is if he begins to show enough progress that she feels he deserves more time. That *is* acceptable.

Are my finances in order?

Now, we're not talking about a reserve trust fund here. I think it's important for you to have put aside enough for you (and any children) to survive for at least three months once you know the relationship is tenuous, at best. You should have already looked into setting up a checking or savings account, and have investigated the possibilities in the job market. This is *in toto* a key question, of course, because if you haven't been able (or willing) to make the necessary preparations, your departure could easily be delayed.

"I had such little money, and I was terrified over how I'd be able to provide for the kids," Sharon said, defending her decision to stay with her husband even though he was showing no change in his behavior. *"What could I do? I couldn't face the possibility that I'd have to give my kids to him. I had to stay."*

I'm not going to deny that for some women, survival on their own is going to be a tough process, especially for those who are unskilled. However, even if things take longer, community colleges and agencies provide short-term training that can support you until you can define or reach long-term goals. Many women have discovered they can get some kind of *financial* support while they are separated from their husbands. It's the *emotional* support they're worried about. Long-term concerns about money certainly are legitimate, but you also have to decide whether to live unhappily, with no hope of emancipation, or in financial circumstances less than ideal.

Have I solicited support from my friends and relatives?

It's generally a good idea to let *some* friends and relatives know about your ultimatum, because if you wind up leaving the man, you can quickly feel tremendous isolation unless there are others on your side. You may have to turn to your parents until you get back on your feet. While friends may not be able to offer financial help, their emotional support will be invaluable during this crucial turning point in your life.

Have my husband and I put the ultimatum in writing?

Putting it in writing makes it carry even more force with the man. Unbelievably, some of these men are shocked when the wife decides to leave. "Why didn't you tell me you were unhappy about this?" Well, of course, she did; he just didn't listen. Or he'll say "I thought you had set a deadline of *next* week." By putting it in writing, you can avoid that lame defense. You can have a fool-proof record of your ultimatum, which is good for you as well as your husband. It almost *forces* you to keep your word—which is what you should be doing anyway.

Have my husband and I tried any type of counseling?

While you may have been seeing a therapist for some time, that's quite different from the *two* of you going together. When the man finally realizes his wife's desperation, when he finally "gets it," he may say "I don't want you to leave. What can I do?" Well, he can agree to therapy early on. Clearly, for years he has been manipulating you and you have allowed it. With your new assertiveness, you have tried to make changes—and maybe he's made some efforts, too. But you've come to the point where it is beyond your abilities to sort out the problems and seek solutions. You need an expert to help the two of you sort things out.

Of course, there is no guarantee that the male partner will be sufficiently committed to the kind of deep introspection that is required to understand his actions. He must see the trail of insecurities, and be willing to depart from it, which is an extremely difficult thing to do. But the woman, if possible, should make every effort to encourage him to enter therapy. Later, even if it doesn't work, they can be content with the knowledge that they did their best.

After they've gone through the aforementioned checklist, women ask me how many of the questions they should answer positively in order to feel free enough to leave their husbands. There is no definitive standard for everyone, but if they've answered most of them affirmatively, then it's probably time to go. The only exception is if they've been physically abused. In that case, all bets are off. Get out immediately, and don't come back!

The separation should be total. Some women decide it's enough to move to another corner of the house, and essentially lead a separate life from their husbands. That won't do it. Only a full physical break from the man will allow the woman to begin her new life. Typically, if the couple has children, the man is the one expected to leave the house, and men usually agree to this without resistance. But if there are no children, usually nothing says the woman can't be the one to find a new place.

The move will not be easy. Frequently, the first thing

that happens is that the women of the Golden Handcuffs begin to replay old tapes, rehashing the childhood memories that had made them so vulnerable in the first place. They start to feel a separation anxiety. They become worried about everything, certain that a catastrophe is about to strike them. These are very similar to the feelings they experienced in childhood. Helen remembers quite well.

"I thought I had it all figured out, and for the first few weeks, life was great when I left Frank. The kids and I were doing fine without him. But then I started to notice that I was getting agitated about everything, and I couldn't stop it. So I decided to see a therapist."

Helen spent the next six months digging deeply into the past that created these anxieties. Unfortunately, not much was gained: She had already known that she was a teenager when her parents divorced, and that the separation from her father had caused her serious pain all through adolescence; she didn't need to spend hard-earned money to figure that out.

As we discussed earlier, the past simply can't be altered. The father who left is not coming back. Women must acknowledge such facts and get on with their lives. In addition, their husbands sense this weakness, this uncertainty, and go in for the kill, exploiting the guilt factor as never before: "Honey, I miss you so much," and "I can't go on without you." The women will begin to feel that leaving their husbands was a huge error—and, believe it or not, many will go back, weaker than ever.

The women also worry about the money. Even though they had put enough away for three months, they start to panic once they see the huge contrast between their old security and their new life of frugality. The man, for all his abusiveness, at least represented a kind of stability in her life. I think it's important for these women to take a pro-active role and see that their rights are granted under the law. Many women listen to their husbands complain about how tough it would be to make payments, and they let them off the hook. That's masochistic. "Better I should suffer (with the children) than he should." That's a rather warped philosophy.

Eventually, as long as the women can survive the initial scares and insecurities, they discover that life as a free person certainly beats a life of indignity. They can function without the man; in fact, they can thrive without him. They can be the women they were supposed to be, not the poor replacement they thought they had to present to the world. Sometimes leaving the man is the only way.

"I moved back to the East Coast," said Nancy, "and it was the right thing. Being in a whole new environment made me feel like it was time to start over. There were no signs of my husband, and I knew I couldn't just jump into my Toyota and go crawling back. I had to get a job. I had to find a new place to live. I had to do everything, and it was about time."

Usually, the first six months are the toughest. That's when all the doubts and insecurities will crop up, sabotaging the most courageous woman's best efforts. But if these women can make it through that period, accepting the anxieties yet refusing to surrender to them, they'll succeed. They will realize that life does not end if their marriage does—and, in fact, it can be even better when they continue to assert themselves thereafter.

CHAPTER EIGHT

Success Stories
From the Golden
Handcuffs Group

Despite a variety of indications to the contrary elucidated
to this point, many women in the Golden Handcuffs are able
to overcome their various home and personal problems and
to salvage their marriages. They make the necessary changes
in their patterns of behavior, and the men reciprocate. (Actually, many men are grateful for the new relationship; they
discover that they never really did like being the master.)
The success stories that follow should encourage the most
pessimistic of women.

Frances, thirty-eight, was married for twenty years, most

of which was quite unpleasant. Her Prince Charming turned into a warden within six months of the ceremony. He never showed her any financial information, and thought he could buy her off whenever she was upset. And he could. But as time went on, Frances began to realize that the temporary euphoria from her shopping trips was wearing off more quickly. They could not remove the pain and isolation that she felt at home. They could not give her the dignity that was missing in her relationship.

Frances fought back. She joined a group, and started to overcome her fears. She admitted that the past could not be changed. She concentrated on the future. Two years after she first sought help, Frances and her husband were sharing financial responsibilities and information. She felt she was an equal partner and did not rehearse statements before she made them to him. She felt free!

"I never thought I could, to be honest with you. I thought I was a prisoner of my past, condemned to the life my mother had, always seeking something that I would never get from a man. I couldn't remember a day that I didn't feel totally miserable, a day where I didn't think of getting in that station wagon and driving off where nobody could ever find me. I dreamed about escaping, but every night I was right where he expected me, making dinner and doing what he wanted.

"Therapy was what finally made me realize that my misery didn't have to be permanent. I had given up on him making all these changes; I realized that I could change, and if he went along with it, great. If not, that didn't mean my life had to be over. I learned how to change, and he resisted for a while. But finally, he understood that he could either jump on the bandwagon, or he was going to find himself alone. He's not

perfect now, but who is? The important thing is that he recognizes me for who I am. I like myself and I like him now, too."

But what about Lisa? She was the woman whose husband practically forced her to wear the bathing suit at the pool party. Did she ever unlock the handcuffs?: You bet she did! And her story is enough to inspire anyone.

"There were so many times I was ready to quit. It was so hard to make progress, to change these lifelong habits I had developed. Even though I kept telling myself one thing, I would fall back into the patterns of weakness and subservience that my husband expected of me. But do you know what finally allowed me to change? Fatigue, that's what. I was so tired of feeling miserable, so tired of being humiliated by the man I thought was going to make my life wonderful. At that point, I frankly didn't care anymore about the consequences. All I knew was that I just couldn't take the pain any more, and I was going to do everything to change that. When you get to that point, it all becomes easy."

Of course, not everyone has to succumb to such desperate straits as Lisa to make the required changes; many women have unlocked the handcuffs long before facing Lisa's kind of life. But what she says is essentially true. The pain of being a second-class citizen in a marriage becomes so intolerable that these women will begin to accomplish things they never imagined possible.

"It was amazing to discover who I was," Karen said. *"All along, here I thought I was weak, that I did deserve eternal unhappiness. For all those years, I thought everything was my fault. It was my fault that my father left my mother. It was my fault that my mother cried all the time, and called me names.*

What I found out was that these things just happened; they weren't my fault. And guess what? I wasn't the weak victim. That wasn't the part I was assigned to play. I was strong, assertive, powerful, and—most of all—happy."

How do women like Frances or Lisa or Karen know exactly when they've unlocked the handcuffs? Is there a moment of true clarity when they understand that they are no longer the women who were so easily manipulated by the Prince Charmings of their lives? Of course not: These changes, as we've described before, take place in small increments over months, sometimes years. But there *are* ways to gauge your progress.

One key indicator that a woman has unlocked the handcuffs is when she finds herself no longer complaining on an almost hourly basis. Before, all she would do was call her friends to report the latest indiscretion, to vent anger that wasn't safe to let out in front of her husband. Suddenly, now she is talking about positive things, about the new and exciting changes she has made in her life. Remember, this won't mean the marriage is any better, but that she has decided to change *her* behavior.

Another sign is when the woman has stopped blaming herself for everything that goes wrong. She starts to see where her responsibility ends, and where her husband's begins. These women have been shouldering far too much blame for the events around them, and that sort of thing has to stop before they can unlock the handcuffs.

How do they keep track of their success? Well, I recommend they compile a "success diary." I tell them that I want them to catalogue only the positive developments in their lives. The negative events aren't necessary, because these will risk reinforcing old patterns of behavior. If they continued to jot down the things they did improperly, many would likely fall back into the familiar vulnerability. They are still far too likely to lean in this direction anyway; the last thing they need is to draw their own road map. They will start to believe whatever bad things they write about themselves.

Instead, the diary should include a daily recounting of all the progressive steps they've taken, such as saying no to the clothing salesman who wanted to sell them one more pair of pants, or spending an hour by themselves without feeling an ounce of guilt, or confronting their husbands without engaging in useless name-calling. I tell the women to write down every single one of these signs of progress.

Naturally, there are going to be setbacks, but even more important than these disappointments is how the women react to them. They can choose to dwell on them, convinced that they represent an inability to make the necessary adjustments. If that's how they feel, then the part of them that wants to sabotage their new image is obviously more powerful than the part that wants a new life. But if they decide they're going to learn from these mistakes, then there is a lot to be hopeful about.

I get phone calls constantly from women who believe that these setbacks represent an emergency. They do not. They are quite normal, and should be treated that way. The women should write down the extent of the setback, and search within themselves for the reasons why it took place. What did they do to contribute to the mistake? And, even more importantly, what can they do to make sure it doesn't happen the next time? It's too late to alter history, but it's the perfect opportunity to chart a better future.

I also ask them to go back to the beginning of the diary and read each page. Only then will they fully understand how far they have come on this journey. In a sense, they are learning how to become their own therapist, how to quickly assimilate the reasons for their behavior without attaching self-destructive judgments. They can learn from every setback.

Yet, no matter how much progress they achieve, one of the most important statements I can make to these women is to remind them that unlocking their handcuffs once does not guarantee they will be free of them for the rest of their lives. Unfortunately, because of their backgrounds, they will *always* be susceptible to Prince Charming sweeping them away into a life of apparent ease and safety. Some will just assume that they picked the wrong man the first time around. What they must remember is that *no* man can act as their savior; they must save themselves. Every day.

These women are similar to alcoholics. Understanding that the Golden Handcuffs syndrome can come back into their lives at any time helps them to avoid going back. Practicing some of the techniques outlined in this book every day can help them to keep these things in mind constantly. The up side is that if they do stay disciplined, they will greatly enhance whatever relationships they enter—and not just those involving their lovers. How they get along with their families and friends will also improve if they respect themselves more, not allowing *anyone* to treat them as doormats.

As such, there is no reason why they have to drop out of support groups, even after they either have mended relations with their husbands, or left them. Again, other women who have faced similar situations can be enormously helpful. Often the key to unlocking the handcuffs is admitting that you may be vulnerable for some time to this pattern of behavior.

Ellen speaks for all those who have made it about what the journey requires.

"I always thought somebody else would have to change before anything got better. I always assumed that I couldn't be the one to do it—but I was wrong. After all, there's nobody else out there who truly cares about your problem as much as you should. You are the one who has to live through the humiliation day after day. You are the one who has to face yourself in the mirror and realize the person you've become. You must decide: What kind of life do I want? Do I want the handcuffs to be wrapped tightly around my wrists for the rest of my life? Or do I want to be free? I wanted to be free, and so I am."

Always remember, your future is in your ability to free yourself from the Golden Handcuffs. A happy and fulfilling life is a long and sometimes difficult journey but the rewards are well worth your efforts.

About the Author

Dr. Neal Olshan is the founder and director of Scottsdale Behavioral Health Center in Scottsdale, Arizona. SBHC is an outpatient treatment center specializing in the evaluation and treatment of depression, anxiety, adult Attention Deficit Disorder, relationship dysfunction, chronic pain and lifestyle change difficulties. Dr. Olshan is in joint practice with his wife, Mary Olshan, M.C., who is a psychotherapist. Dr. Neal Olshan has founded and directed inpatient and outpatient programs in clinical and hospital settings. He is an advisor to national organizations involved in the areas of psychology and rehabilitation. Dr. Olshan and his wife live in Phoenix, Arizona and have three children.

About the Author

[illegible] Scottsdale, Arizona [illegible] in the evaluation and [illegible] Attention Deficit [illegible]